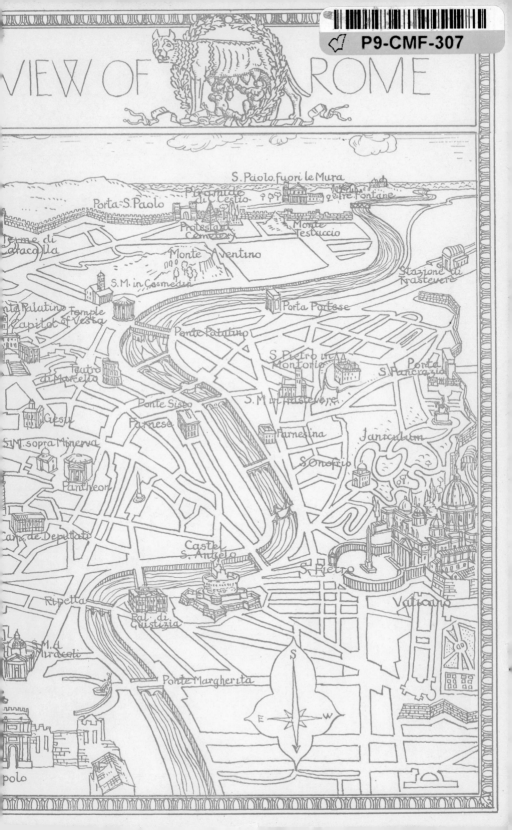

VIEW OF ROME

A WANDERER
IN ROME

E. V. LUCAS

Other Books of E. V. LUCAS

ENTERTAINMENTS

ADVISORY BEN
GENEVRA'S MONEY
ROSE AND ROSE
VERENA IN THE MIDST
THE VERMILION BOX
LANDMARKS
LISTENER'S LURE
MR. INGLESIDE
OVER BEMERTON'S
LONDON LAVENDER

ESSAYS

LUCK OF THE YEAR
GIVING AND RECEIVING
ROVING EAST AND ROVING
  WEST
ADVENTURES AND ENTHUSI-
  ASMS
CLOUD AND SILVER
A BOSWELL OF BAGHDAD
TWIX EAGLE AND DOVE
THE PHANTOM JOURNAL
LOITERER'S HARVEST
ONE DAY AND ANOTHER
FIRESIDE AND SUNSHINE
CHARACTER AND COMEDY
OLD LAMPS FOR NEW

TRAVEL

A WANDERER IN ROME
A WANDERER AMONG PIC-
  TURES
A WANDERER IN VENICE
A WANDERER IN PARIS
A WANDERER IN LONDON
A WANDERER IN HOLLAND
A WANDERER IN FLORENCE
MORE WANDERINGS IN LON-
  DON
HIGHWAYS AND BYWAYS IN
  SUSSEX

EDITED WORKS

THE WORKS OF CHARLES
  AND MARY LAMB
THE HAUSFRAU RAMPANT

ANTHOLOGIES

THE OPEN ROAD
THE FRIENDLY TOWN
HER INFINITE VARIETY
GOOD COMPANY
THE GENTLEST ART
THE SECOND POST
THE BEST OF LAMB
REMEMBER LOUVAIN

BOOKS FOR CHILDREN

PLAYTIME & COMPANY
THE SLOWCOACH
ANNE'S TERRIBLE GOOD NA-
  TURE
A BOOK OF VERSES FOR
  CHILDREN
ANOTHER BOOK OF VERSES
  FOR CHILDREN
RUNAWAYS AND CASTAWAYS
FORGOTTEN STORIES OF LONG
  AGO
MORE FORGOTTEN STORIES
THE "ORIGINAL VERSES" OF
  ANN AND JANE TAYLOR

BIOGRAPHY

THE LIFE OF CHARLES LAMB
A SWAN AND HER FRIENDS
THE BRITISH SCHOOL
THE HAMBLEDON MEN

SELECTED WRITINGS

A LITTLE OF EVERYTHING
HARVEST HOME
VARIETY LANE
MIXED VINTAGES

A WANDERER
IN ROME

BY

E. V. LUCAS

WITH SIXTEEN ILLUSTRATIONS IN COLOUR BY

HARRY MORLEY

AND THIRTY-TWO REPRODUCTIONS FROM PHOTOGRAPHS

"Go thou to Rome, at once the Paradise,
The Grave, The City and the Wilderness."

SHELLEY (*Adonais*)

GEORGE H. DORAN COMPANY
On Murray Hill : : New York

PREFACE

Rome was not built in a day, and it cannot be seen in one—at least not thoroughly; but English people ought to know that it can be reached from London in a little more than that brief division of time. Only one night in the train does the journey involve. I doubt if this fact is generally recognized. More people would go to Rome if it were.

I cannot enumerate the many books which I have consulted in order to write this one. There would not be space. But I must express my indebtedness to many predecessors.

E. V. L.

May, 1926.

CONTENTS

vii

CONTENTS

LIST OF PICTURES

In Colour

LIST OF ILLUSTRATIONS

In Monotone

A WANDERER
IN ROME

A WANDERER IN ROME

CHAPTER I

The Impact of Rome

Where to begin one's Wanderings—The Puzzle of North and South—The Porta del Popolo—Outside the Railway Station—Ancient and Modern rub Shoulders—The Temple of Minerva Medica.— S. Bibiana.

WHERE to begin one's wanderings in Rome?—that is a question which it has troubled me to answer.

The railway station is a natural spot, especially as Rome has but one that counts. But against it is the fact that the line which brings most of Rome's visitors hither describes such a curve that, although most of these visitors are coming from the north, they actually enter Rome from the south. This means that it takes a long time to recover the lost orientation.

Years ago, before the railway came, the Porta del Popolo, Rome's northern entrance by road, was the true starting-point; and indeed I think it is still almost the best. Certainly so for motorists. To begin with, ancient cities should be approached through gates, and this gate is a noble one; while from it start no fewer than four arterial streets.

First, the Corso Umberto I, or *the* Corso, running nearly due south between the twin churches and ending in

15

the golden and glistening splendours of the new Vittorio Emmanuele II Memorial, backing against the ancient Capitol.

Secondly, obliquely to the right of the entrance to the Corso, the Via Ripetta—which in time, and under changes of name, comes to the Pantheon and so through busy parts of old Rome to the Tiber, at the Ponte Garibaldi, and then to Trastevere.

Thirdly, immediately on the right, with an entrance at each side of the garden, the Via Ferdinando di Savoia, which at once crossing the Tiber at the Ponte Margherita runs into the Via Cola di Rienzi and so straight to the Vatican and St. Peter's.

And fourthly, the street to the left of the left church at the entrance to the Corso, the Via del Babuino, which runs to the Piazza di Spagna and so on to the Via Nazionale through the tunnel beneath the King's palace and gardens. From this Via del Babuino, by a deflection to the left just past the Piazza di Spagna, the Via Sistina is gained, which runs up hill and down to the great church of S. Maria Maggiore, or, at the Four Fountains, lets you into the Via Venti Settembre.

So you see that the Porta del Popolo is a real starting-point, and, for visitors arriving by road, the most natural of all. None the less, I am proposing to begin most of these rambles at the Piazza di Spagna, for the reason that that is a central spot in itself and also the favourite meeting-place of English and Americans. English is heard sporadically all over Rome, whether on St. Peter's dome or in the depths of the catacombs, but in the Piazza di Spagna it may be said to be the only tongue. For the Piazza di Spagna has the libraries, the tourist bureaus, the tea rooms; it is the capital of the artists' colony; it has antiquity shops and apartment agents; it is close to the Pincio with its gardens and views, and it is one of the

VIEW FROM THE PINCIO, WITH S. CARLO AL CORSO MOST PROMINENT

[*See page* 20

parts of old Rome nearest to the new Ludovisi quarter with the fashionable hotels in the latest manner and the elegant and sumptuous flats.

From the Piazza di Spagna we will therefore make it a habit to set forth.

Before we begin, however, I should like to say a word more about the railway station, lest I may appear to be slighting it. That is far from the case, for the Rome terminus is almost unique. No city can divulge all its secrets instantly to the arriving guest; but some have their railway stations in such remote positions that you must drive for many minutes before you are in characteristic streets at all; while some, like London, have a large choice, each of which is in a different district. Rome, however, has but one, and no sooner do you step outside it than Rome, essential Rome, begins: for you have before your eyes a remnant of the wall of Servius, built in the fifth century B.C.; and the Terme, or Baths, of the Emperor Diocletian, dating from the fourth century A.D. with the sixteenth century church of S. Maria degli Angeli, one of the works of Michael Angelo, rising from their midst; while at the opening of the Via Nazionale the Esedra, or crescent of modern white buildings, is fully representative of the Roman architecture of to-day. In the open space in front of Michael Angelo's church is a memorial of the Great War of 1914-1918, and here also is one of Rome's many high-spirited fountains, with its naiads and gods and its glittering column of waters so often bent and dispersed by the wind. This fountain and its buoyant crystal flow together illustrate very vividly the mixture of old and new of which I am speaking. The fountain dates from 1900; the water comes from the Sabine Hills along the very aqueduct built in 146 B.C. by the Prætor Quintus Marcius Rex.

I don't say that this astonishing jumble of old and

new is as exciting to the stranger as, at Venice, outside the railway station, the instantaneous and magical appearance of the Grand Canal; but it should be inspiring enough, and the mixed anachronistic character of the first impression of Rome, as one emerges from the terminus, will persist. Wherever you go in Rome, you will find the ages in conflict: from B.C. onwards. You will attend divine service in churches adapted from pagan temples; you will eat, at the Ulpia, the food of to-day in the remains of a basilica built in the reign of Trajan; you will ride in tramcars through the gates of the crumbling city wall; you will smoke cigarettes in the Colosseum; listen to the latest music in the Augusteum, now a concert hall, but originally the mausoleum of the great Augustus; and find advertisements bearing the names of cinema stars pasted against stones that Cicero may have seen the builders setting one on the other.

As to the railway itself, when it was made in the middle of the last century, it cut through very sacred ground, as you see when you ride along the Viale Principessa Margherita, the road beside the line, to the Porta Maggiore and thence into the Campagna. It is just by the Porta Maggiore that the line pierces the Wall of Aurelian, and, a little later, Nero's aqueduct has to be negotiated. The decagonal building in the Viale Principessa Margherita is the so-called Temple of Minerva Medica, a nymphæum or marriage-hall, dating from the great imperial days.

The church on the left before we reach this ruin is S. Bibiana. Here in the fourth century stood the house of Flavian, a prefect and a Christian, who with his wife and two daughters, Demetria and Bibiana, suffered martyrdom in the brief return to paganism under Julian. The story is that Bibiana was tied to the porphyry pillar which is still preserved in the church, and scourged to death. Her statue over the high altar is by Bernini.

THE IMPACT OF ROME

The shortest route to the church of S. Lorenzo where, as we shall see, Pius IX is buried, is by the road that branches off just here and goes under the railway.

If the reader of these pages finds that they also are an undisciplined mixture of old and new, he should not express either surprise or censure, because I have allowed Rome to call the tune. If Rome is of all ages at once, so must the record be. I will concede, however, that perhaps *A Digresser in Rome* would have been a better title.

Chapter II

The Pincio and the Villa Medici

Michael Angelo and Daniele da Volterra—The French Academy—
Galileo—Corot in Rome—Turner in Italy—The Avenues of Busts—
Rome from the Pincio Terrace—The Costumes of the Seminarists—
And of the Monks.

WHATEVER formal expeditions one makes from the Piazza di Spagna, the habit of informally strolling in the Pincio gardens must be quickly contracted. The Pincio is not one of the Seven Hills of Rome, but for long lay outside the city; its name coming from the Pincii, a ruling family who had their palace there.

The obelisk at the head of the steps, erected by Hadrian before the tomb of Antinous, was moved hither early in the nineteenth century, but why it was set askew I cannot explain. The church behind it, the Santissima Trinità de' Monti, is not as accessible as most of Rome's churches are, but visitors are admitted if they apply at a side door. Its chief artistic attraction is a picture by Daniele da Volterra, a bold draughtsman whose principal title to fame is his close friendship with that most difficult of men, Michael Angelo. The sculptured head of the Master in the Accademia in Florence, by which we know him best, with the broken nose and the profoundly melancholy eyes, was from Daniele da Volterra's hand. The two men worked together in Rome. The Volterra altar-piece has no outstanding merit; better to stand in the pretty cloisters and watch the pupils of a convent school at

THE PINCIO AND THE VILLA MEDICI

play, for too seldom does one see Rome in a playful mood.

After leaving the church, turning to the right towards the Pincio gardens, which is the most popular walking place in Rome for those who like air and open spaces (the most popular for the Romans themselves will always be the streets, and chiefly the Corso Umberto I), we come at once to the famous Villa Medici. Built in the sixteenth century for Cardinal Ricci, it was acquired by Cardinal Alessandro de' Medici, who became Pope Leo XI in 1605, and thereafter for two hundred years was the property of the later Medici, the Grand Dukes of Tuscany. Since 1803 it has been the French Academy of Art, and to mention even the names of the well-known French artists who have studied here would fill a volume. It has some original reliefs built into its walls—six from the Ara Pacis, of which we shall see fragments at the Terme of Diocletian and of which the Uffizi in Florence has a roomfull—but the collection of casts is the chief possession. Admission to the casts and to the gardens is given on certain days. It was in these gardens that Velasquez, when in Rome in 1630, made the two beautiful—and so very modern—landscapes that are now among the glories of the Prado.

The principal historical event in the life of the Villa was the imprisonment here of Galileo, as a tablet records on a pillar at the entrance to the sloping drive down to the Porta del Popolo. This was in 1633, when the great astronomer and mathematician was nearly seventy and had fallen foul of the Inquisition for the dangerous, antibiblical theories contained in his treatise on the earth's motion. The old philosopher, standing in the church of S. Maria sopra Minerva, had read his recantation, denying that he was a naughty Copernican, but sentence followed.

The gardens are typically Italian: very dark boskage, mostly evergreen, contrasting with the whiteness of statues and the yellow wash of walls. Here and there is a studio; here and there a tablet commemorating an Art director. Winners of the Prix de Rome have free study here, but not a sign of their work do you see. Only the frigid casts from the antique. A diploma gallery of votive pictures by all the prize-winners would be an interesting addition.

Immediately in front of the Villa Medici door is a fountain in a shallow basin set in an opening in the thick and carefully trimmed ilexes. Standing by the Villa and looking over this fountain you see two domes of churches —one straight ahead, and one more to the right. The first is S. Carlo in the Corso and the other St. Peter's. Many artists have painted this view of St. Peter's, but none so well as Corot, who was in Rome from 1825 to 1828. The original, of which I give a reproduction, is in the late Sir Hugh Lane's collection in his house in Dublin, now that city's Municipal Art Gallery.

Corot's Roman pictures, of which we have one in the National Gallery, are not very numerous, and they belong to his harder manner before the mists gathered. But his contemporary Turner, who was here first in 1819, and again in 1829 and 1839, made thousands of sketches, a few of which were worked up into paintings and others were etched. It was while on the journey from Rome to Bologna in a diligence that a fellow-passenger noticed the "funny little elderly gentleman continuously sketching at the window, and angry at the conductor for not waiting while he took a sketch of a sunrise at Macerata. 'D—— the fellow!' he said, 'he has no feeling.' " Some of Turner's Italian water-colours are lovely beyond description; but I think that even more of the romantic feeling of the surroundings of Rome is to be found in certain work by his indirect master J. R. Cozens, whose studies of Lake Nemi, once seen, can never be forgotten.

Keeping the upper path by the Villa Medici among cacti and other sub-tropical plants you come quickly to the restaurant, a very pleasant spot in summer, in the midst of a concourse of terminal figures, lining all the paths hereabouts, each bearing the bust of a famous Italian. This marble Valhalla was the idea of Mazzini. The earliest hero, I believe, is Julius Cæsar; of the latest you will know more than I, for to this august company of the distinguished dead recruits are constant. Among the new ones are a few dazzlingly white marble heads, some of young men whom the gods loved too well. Modern critics may scribble in pencil on their pedestals; but of old they broke noses. Too many of the ancient Romans are without that organ; even Cavour's has gone. But after Cavour more respect seems to have come in. In English churches we expect to find statues thus mutilated; but not in Rome, where you would think the nose sacred.

To see now one of the finest views of Rome we should keep to the path at the edge of the hill, with the pomegranates below us under the walls, and the skilfully tended gardens below those, and the ilexes above us, until we come to the terrace over the Piazza del Popolo. From many points on her surrounding hills Rome is serene and impressive, but never more so than here from the Pincio. St. Peter's is immense, and at least eight little imitations of it can be counted. The Courts of Justice are out of scale, you will notice, and the bulk of the new Vittorio Emmanuele II monument obliterates too much. Observe how the strange shallow dome of the Pantheon catches the eye. The Archangel Michael on his Castello is cut in two by the horizon.

It is a favourite spot at sunset, and sunsets at Rome

can be very wonderful: "stained with the blood of martyrs," some one said.

For the Pincio as a park and promenade Rome has to thank Pius VII, who ordained this pleasure realm early in the nineteenth century. In cold weather it is perfect to walk in, and in warm weather perfect for repose. Here beneath the trees the band plays, gaily-clad foster-mothers nourish babes, nurses gossip while their olive-faced charges play, elegant young Romans discuss the events of the hour, lovers keep their happy rendezvous.

But the principal memory that the observant eye gathers in the Pincio gardens is that of the constantly recurring little bands of seminarists, with their splashes of colour, who walk briskly along on their way to and from the wider spaces of the Villa Umberto I chatting gaily together. You meet them everywhere in Rome, but never so steadily as here or on the Scala di Spagna, descending or ascending according to the time of day, the wind taking their skirts like those of Niobe's daughter in the Vatican. Brightest if not best of these sons of the church are the Germans—all in cardinal red: the only ones to get a footing on the picture postcards.

Having often been struck by the variety of their costumes, and too often when drawing near having been baffled by an inability to catch their voices (for, as every one must have noticed, while there are moments on the Continent when every one seems to be talking English, there are months when they most emphatically do not), I here subjoin, for the benefit of other normally inquisitive persons, a list of the principal distinguishing colours. Thus, when you see all scarlet it is the Germans; when all black, the English; black edged with red and no sash, the Irish; a purple cassock with black soprana and crimson sash, the Scotch. Americans from the States are black edged with blue and a red sash; South Americans, black

THE PIAZZA DEL POPOLO, WITH S. MARIA DEI MIRACOLI
AND S. MARIA IN MONTE SANTO

[*See page* 23

lined with blue and blue sash; Belgians have a black cassock and soprana and sash bordered with red; the French are all black with black soprana fastened round the neck with long black ribbons; Canadians are black, with belt; Spanish, black, with blue buttons and blue sash; Greeks, dark blue with a red sash. The Vatican students have purple cassocks and crimson sashes, and those at the Propaganda College, black, edged with red and red sashes. The umbrella is rarely left at home.

Perhaps a list of the costumes of the religious orders would also be helpful. The Italian Augustinians are in black with a white cord; the Irish Augustinians are in black with a hooded cloak; the Benedictines are in black with large sleeves; the Order of St. Camillus wear black with a large red cross on the breast; the Capuchins are in brown with a cape (the colour of café au lait, which therefore is called a "capucino" in the restaurants); the Carmelites brown with white cloak; the Cistercians white; the Dominicans white with black cloak; the Franciscans brown; the Jesuits black; the Passionists black with badge of the Passion; the Redemptorists black with white collar; the Servites black with hooded cloak; the Silvestrians blue; the Trinitarians white with large red or blue cross; the Brothers of the Immaculate Conception light blue with white cord.

Chapter III

The Piazza di Spagna and the Fontana di Trevi

A City of Fountains—The Famous Steps—Flower-stalls and Artists' Models—John Keats in Rome—His Last Days—Shelley and Byron—The Protestant Cemetery—Angelica Kauffmann—Sir Walter Scott—The Aqua Virgo—The Fontana di Trevi—An Essential Ceremony.

THE Piazza di Spagna takes its name from the palace at the west side, the Palazzio di Spagna, the Spanish Embassy to the Vatican. Between the palace and the little piazza opposite (at the corner of which the tramcars, always of homicidal intent in Rome, do their best to get you) rises a column celebrating the doctrine of the Immaculate Conception of the Virgin, which the Church of Rome adopted in 1854. The building at the south end is the Collegio di Propaganda, which is attended by youths from all over the world whose destiny it is to spread the Church of Rome's tenets.

The Piazza di Spagna, like so many of Rome's open spaces, of course has its fountain, and almost equally of course the fountain was designed by Bernini, who chose the emblem of a waterlogged boat as a hint to the authorities that the supply of water in his house, close by, at the corner of the Via della Mercede and the Via di Propaganda, lacked impetus. Of Bernini, whose head you will see on a tablet on his house, I shall have much to say later. Here let me merely remark that in his versatility and his energy as an architect, if not in genius, he resembled the great Michael Angelo, whom he succeeded as builder-in-chief to the Eternal City.

26

THE SCALA DI SPAGNA FROM THE VIA CONDOTTI

[*See page* 27

THE PIAZZA DI SPAGNA

It is probably a good deal due to Bernini that Rome is a city of fountains as well as of churches, fine buildings and ruins; and these fountains, moreover, are always playing. We have few fountains in London, and how often even those are lifeless! In Trafalgar Square, for instance, where you would think that, in honour of Nelson alone, they might be kept busy, they are seldom in full flow; while the Queen Victoria Memorial, opposite Buckingham Palace, is often dry. But in Rome there is a gushing fountain every few yards. For size and spirit and energy the modern Fontana delle Naiadi, near the station, is among the best, but the Fontana di Trevi remains longest in the memory. We will hasten there very soon.

The best known feature of the Piazza di Spagna is of course its steps: that gracious curved staircase so warmly yellow in the evening sun, with the warmly yellow church at its summit also cherishing the dying light. From the lower end of the Via Condotti, and farther back still, in the Via Fontanella di Borghese, the twin domes of this church often seem to hang in the sky. At the foot of the steps are the famous flower-sellers with their blossoms. All the year they are here, with changing blooms, oddly enough making almost their bravest show when the weather is coldest. Here also are artists' models seeking employers. You may know the men by their pictorial hair and also by their umbrellas.

All Italy is devoted to the umbrella, but no city (and with some reason) more than Rome, where rain, when it does fall, rains heavily and patiently and pitilessly, and where in the Corso Umberto I is an admirable institution called an Albergo Diurno, or daytime inn (with several branches), at which, for a few pence and a deposit, umbrellas may be hired for short periods.

As the number of the Piazza di Spagna steps is said to be one hundred and thirty-seven it may be glad tidings

27

that there is a lift. It is just round the corner at the back of Miss Wilson's English library (that home-for-home for so many Anglo-Saxons in Rome), and, in addition to supplying motive power to deposit you with an unquickened pulse at the summit of the flight, the custodian will give you a time-table of the opening and closing hours of all the show places of Rome, without which you cannot arrange your days.

Before ascending, however, we must take stock of the house on the right of the steps, which has a tablet on its red wall, with a broken lyre upon it. A tragic house, indeed, for it was the last home of John Keats.

Keats's association with Italy began in 1820, when he was twenty-five and the symptoms of consumption were distressingly on the increase. Between March 1818 and the autumn of 1819 he had written his finest work, the poetry in the "Lamia," "Isabella" and "Eve of St. Agnes" volume. This was published in 1820, and shortly afterwards Keats started for Naples, with his friend Joseph Severn, on the ship *Maria Crowther*. The date of sailing was September 18, 1820. The winds being adverse, the voyage took nearly a month, followed by ten days' quarantine at Naples, but Rome, where Severn, who had won the Royal Academy gold medal, was to study painting, was reached in November. Shelley, who was then at Pisa, asked Keats to join him there; but the Eternal City was the goal.

Lodgings in this house on the Piazza di Spagna steps had been taken for the friends by Keats's doctor, James, afterwards Sir James, Clark, and here almost at once a relapse set in, from which the poet never really rallied. Apart from his physical suffering, he was torn by a lover's fears and doubts, for the vacillating Fanny Brawne was ever in his mind. Severn nursed him with perfect devotion, sometimes reading, Jeremy Taylor being a favourite author, sometimes playing Haydn's sonatas. On February 23, 1821, the poet's "posthumous life," as he whimsically called it, came to a close.

Keats died in the little room looking out on the flower-sellers, and the house is now a museum filled with books and papers and pictures relating to the poet and to his friends Shelley, Byron, Leigh Hunt, and Severn. There is not much in the way of original MSS.: those are elsewhere, in England and America; but the library is extensive and some personal relics are preserved. Keats is, of course, the central character; but Shelley, who, when in Rome, lived in the Corso, runs him very close. A bone from Shelley's funeral pyre is here, and strands of his hair are shown. There is also an original picture, by Severn, of the author of "Adonais" "meditating in the Baths of Caracalla," just as a poet should. Byron's lodgings were in the Piazza di Spagna, almost opposite. "Cet aimable boiteux" he is called in one of the letters to be seen in this museum—and how he would have hated it!

The Protestant cemetery in Rome is a long way from the Piazza di Spagna, but since the graves of Keats and Shelley make it sacred ground to so many Anglo-Saxon pilgrims, I think I should say something of it in this place. You find it by the Porta di S. Paolo, where the road runs out past factories to the mighty fane of St. Paul. Many are the graves, of all nationalities, but there are none to compare in interest with those of the two poets—of "Adonais" and of his celebrant. Beside Shelley, whose heart alone is here, lies the berserk Trelawney, who, on the shore at Spezzia, plucked that heart from the burning. Some one had placed carnations on Shelley's grave when I was there; and there were carnations also at the foot of the stone which marks the last resting-place of the "young English poet," whose name was "writ in water." It is odd that the word Keats is absent; but

A WANDERER IN ROME

I had not thought so until another visitor, standing beside me, asked if I could tell him who the poor young man might be.

Another English writer, not of the same rank, but a great bestower of pleasure on the young, is buried here— "Ballantyne the brave"—but I have never been able to find the stone. Shelley's little son, William, who died at the age of three, also lies in this earth. The pyramid rising so oddly at the edge of the grassy plot where Keats and Severn lie is the tomb of Caius Cestius, a tribune, who died in the first century B.C.

And now we must go quickly to the Fontana di Trevi. If you leave the Piazza di Spagna at the south end to the right of the Collegio di Propaganda, you are in the Via di Propaganda, which brings you to the church of Saint' Andrea delle Fratte (St. Andrew of the Fences or Hedges), with its very memorable belfry. This church was the natural resort of Scottish pilgrims to Rome in the Middle Ages; but it is not now an important place of pilgrimage except for those who remember Miss Thackeray's delightful novel *Miss Angel*, for Angelica Kauffmann, R.A. (1741-1807), is buried here. After a successful artistic, although chequered emotional, career, in England, Angelica Kauffmann settled in Rome and remained there for the last twenty-five years of her life; and when she died her funeral was stage-managed by Canova, two of her works were carried in procession and all the artists in Rome followed.

A greater than Angelica, Sir Walter Scott, lodged at No. 11 Via della Mercede in 1832, one of the reasons for this journey, so near his end, being to see the monument of the last of the Stuarts in St. Peter's. It is sad that that very fine record of a great man, Scott's *Journal*, stops at the moment that he reached Rome.

Next door to St. Andrew's, on the left of the façade,

30

is the entrance to a little cloistered building which, once
a Scottish hospice, is now an almshouse for sailors. One
does not expect to find this in Rome, although years ago
the Tiber was a port for big ships.

If, after leaving St. Andrew of the Hedges, you follow
his street, you will come into the Via del Nazareno. Keep
to the left as far as the Via del Tritone, cross that, and
take the Via della Stamperia, and in the Piazza at the end
of it pause, because this is one of the most important spots
in Rome, especially to travellers from abroad like ourselves—for here is the Fontana di Trevi.

Any fountain, so long as it is playing, must be beautiful
—the lithe and silvery stream ensures that; but the
Roman fountains have beauty of design too. This Fontana di Trevi is, however, different from all the others:
in position, built as it is against a palace wall, the Palazzo
Poli; in tradition; in size; and in flow. It is not so very
old, having been completed in 1762, but there had been
an outlet of water here for centuries: the Aqua Virgo, a
stream brought into Rome from the Campagna by
Agrippa in 19 B.C. to supply his baths near the Pantheon. The Virgo was the country girl at work in the
Campagna who showed Agrippa's engineers where the
spring bubbled; the new name Trevi means three ways,
referring to the three main outlets of the fountain to-
day: one in the middle, under the statue of Neptune, and
the others at the sides, beneath the figures of Health
and Fertility. These main streams are broken by the
rocks into a score of minor torrents which in their total
exuberance make one of the coolest and most delicious
melodies of Rome.

But not yet have we learned the deepest significance
of this cataract. If you look carefully into the placid
water of the pool, you will discern at the bottom (provided
that the expectant urchins have not yet pulled them out)

various small coins. These have been thrown into it in accordance with the legend which says that the sacrifice of a coin to the waters of Trevi ensures your return to the Eternal City. If you wait here a little while (after making your own oblation) you will see other visitors approach with the same motive, some furtively, some unashamed.

Reproduced by kind permission of the Curator

OME, FROM THE PINCIO
After the picture by COROT *in the Municipal Gallery of Modern Art, Dublin*

[*See page* 22

MONUMENT TO CARDINAL GIROLAMO BASSO DELLA ROVERE
By ANDREA SANSOVINO in the Church of
S. Maria del Popolo

[See page 35

CHAPTER IV

The Piazza del Popolo and the Corso

The northern Gate—Rome's Obelisks—Raphael's Chapel—Tuscan
Tombs—Twin Churches—The Corso—The arrogant Roman—The
Tomb of Augustus—S. Carlo Borromeo—The Caffé Nazionale—
The Temple of the Sun—S. Silvestro—Marcus Aurelius's Column—
A Miracle—St. Paul's Residence—The Roman Palaces—Velasquez's
Pope—Claude in Rome—A Royal Memorial—Vittorio Emmanuele
II—The Unknown Warrior—Views of Rome—The Pantheon.

A N early walk from the Piazza di Spagna should take
you down the Via del Babuino to the Porta del
Popolo, which was, as I have said, the principal gateway
through which, before the railway came, Rome was entered. It was built in 1562, on the site of an older gate
in Aurelian's Wall. Bernini added the Piazza façade;
while the Porta's two side apertures were an affair of
yesterday—1878. Outside the gate you will always find
many of the high narrow wine-carts of the Campagna
with little noisy restless yapping *lupetti* guarding them
while their owners gossip in the neighbouring inns. These
carts are a feature of Rome and the surrounding country, and their gay hoods give the streets much of their
colour, which otherwise is supplied chiefly by fruit shops,
scarves, and the red pompons and tassels on the horses'
harness. On every road out of Rome you find these high
and rickety vehicles—after lunch with the drivers asleep,
the whole duty of avoiding other traffic falling upon their
loyal steeds.

In the centre of the Piazza del Popolo is the fountain
with four lions, with an Egyptian obelisk in their midst,

33

first set up in the Circus Maximus by the Emperor Augustus, ten years before the birth of Christ. These obelisks are constantly recurring in Rome's open spaces, and never with any suggestion of incongruity, so skilfully have they been adapted to their settings. Even the little one on the back of an elephant opposite S. Maria sopra Minerva seems right.

The church immediately to the left of the gate as you face Rome, is S. Maria del Popolo, and it is important, not only for having been built on the site of Nero's grave, for the purpose (in which it was successful) of exorcising the evil-working demons that collected there, but also as containing an exquisite chapel designed by Raphael in one of his rare architectural moods—the Cappella Chigi, with a statue of Jonah emerging from a very trivial Leviathan, also by Raphael, in one of the niches by the altar. The altar-piece by Sebastian del Piombo you cannot see; whereas the altar-piece by Pinturicchio on the opposite side of the church is both visible and charming. We shall find this happy painter again in Rome, notably in the Borgia Apartments at the Vatican, but never quite so gay as in Siena.

The Agostino Chigi who commissioned Raphael was a wealthy banker, a Sienese, whose financial assistance more than one Pope found invaluable. He was a power behind the scenes through the reigns of Julius II and Leo X, and he died five days after his beloved Raphael, in 1520, and had a funeral almost unsurpassed in splendour. The carved portrait on his pyramidal tomb shows him to have been handsome and debonair.

The special treasures of this little church, after Raphael's chapel, are the tombs, all of which are of sensitive Tuscan work too rarely found in this city of baroque, and here are in a Bernini baroque setting which, to my eyes, makes them by contrast the more welcome. The

34

masterpieces are the tomb of Cardinal Cristoforo della Rovere by Mino da Fiesole and Andrea Bregno, in the first chapel in the right aisle (decorated by Pinturicchio), and in the choir, also decorated by Pinturicchio, the two tombs of Cardinals by Andrea Sansovino.

After leaving Raphael's church we may cross the Piazza and walk along the famous Corso. But first look high up to the left, where you will always see a few people on the terrace above the loggia where Vittorio Emmanuele II sits his horse, showing each other the view. Beneath is the winding road to the Pincio among the trees, and on the fountain at the foot of the hill is the first representation of Romulus and Remus and their foster-mother which the traveller entering Rome from the north would see.

The twin churches at the entrance to the Corso are, on the right, S. Maria de' Miracoli, and on the left, S. Maria in Monte Santo. Neither has any special treasure. Both the porticos, each surmounted by a pediment, were constructed of stone from Bernini's belfry at St. Peter's, which fell. Concerning these churches a pretty story is told, to the effect that a poor woman in her will left her few pence towards their completion, and that Pope Alexander VII, one of the Chigi family, hearing of this, took it upon himself to see her last wishes more than carried out.

We now enter the famous Corso, which is so called because it was once the scene of exciting horse-races, and even to-day the line of motor cars is now and then romantically broken by a trotting horse flinging out its feet and straining at the reins on its way to a country track. As for the motor cars, at certain hours they practically touch each other, all hooting incessantly and with peculiarly offensive notes. If you do as Rome does, you will pay no attention whatever, for the Romans have more than the usual Latin indifference to noise. Even when trams clang and clatter and scream through the narrowest streets, they are unmoved. You never see them hurry out of the way; but also you never see them run over. Like the men of Sussex (whose proud boast was perhaps derived from Julius Cæsar's invading legions), they "won't be druv."

Motor cars being allowed in Rome's narrowest alleys, there is almost no place safe from them; and the notice saying that they must proceed only "at the pace of a man," being an official order, is disregarded. The builders of Rome present, indeed, an odd paradox: they made palaces for giants and roads for pigmies.

A reason for the constant hooting is the absence of any rule of the road in the city. Direction is dependent entirely upon the quickness of the drivers' brains and their sense of give and take. No collisions in Rome have I seen, but I confess to having been made exceedingly nervous when, in a fast car, the chauffeur has relied solely upon the arrogant movements of his imperious Roman head or of his imperious Roman hand to indicate to others what course he was intending to steer. We in England spend not a little breath in proclaiming our freedom, but there is a deeper sense of independence and individuality in Rome than one ever notices in London.

I may say here that the visitor to this city of Seven Hills who does not walk is in some difficulty of choice between the over-speeded motor car on the one hand, and on the other the under-horsed carriage. What Rome— and indeed every place—now wants is a half-speed car, the occupant of which has a chance of seeing something, and the driver of which is sufficiently detached from the machine to be stoppable on impulse.

At first the Corso is drab and not in the least remarkable, except for the fact, so evident in all but the newest parts of Rome, that behind every door is a crowded past.

PIAZZA DEL POPOLO AND THE CORSO

For in Rome the past is always present. Every building either bears traces of previous existences, or you are aware of them. When the Porta del Popolo, for example, was known as the Porta Flaminia, the Corso was the Via Lata, with togas where you now see coats; while only a few yards from the main street where we now move was the mausoleum built for his family by the Emperor Augustus in B.C. 28. A concert hall to-day occupies the site.

The two churches which we soon come to are modest, with façades in a line with the houses and shops: on the left Gesù è Maria, where Cardinal Wiseman used to preach, and on the right S. Giacomo in Augusta, the chapel of the adjoining hospital, often visited by St. Philip Neri. St. Philip lived at S. Maria in Vallicella, in the Corso Vittorio Emmanuele, where his rooms and his tomb and Guido Reni's portrait of him may be seen.

A very different church is S. Carlo al Corso, the great florid edifice on the right, to which we now come, dedicated to S. Carlo Borromeo, whose heart is preserved here. Like so many of Rome's churches, this one would make a very creditable cathedral in England. The chief altarpiece, by Carlo Maratta, depicts S. Carlo, or St. Charles, being presented by the Madonna to her Son. Maratta (1625-1713) you will find to be one of the favourite painters in Roman churches, although he and his companions of the decline no longer stand where they did. S. Carlo Borromeo, I might say, was on very friendly terms with English churchmen, and was hospitable to many exiles forced by the Reformation to leave our country.

You will find some essential Rome, overcrowded and not too clean, at the back of S. Carlo, and in a cell under the church a cobbler has made his home. Some little rooms have even been built high up against the church walls, as, in England, little pieces of common land used to be encroached upon by cottages. In Holland this juxta-position of church and shop and residence is almost normal; but one seldom finds it in Italy.

It is at the Via Condotti, leading up the Piazza di Spagna (you will see the steps and the church at the top) that the Corso begins to be lively. A little farther along, at the junction of the Via della Vite, was once an arch corresponding to London's Temple Bar, and removed for the same reason, that it interfered with the traffic. This was the arch of Marcus Aurelius.

By the time we reach the Caffè Nazionale, or Peroni and Aragno's, the Corso is populous indeed, chiefly with men, for the Bourse and Houses of Parliament are adjacent, and you will quickly get an idea of the modern Roman type. Middle-aged and elderly men being for the moment disregarded, I may say that there is something very attractive in the typical young Roman's lean straight figure, his keen eagle-like features and high sloped forehead; even in his general air of being sure that he is the best. The likeness of these young men to one another is very remarkable. Most of them in pairs would seem to be brothers.

You will soon observe too, no matter how odd may be your clothes, that the Romans do not resemble other Latins in the matter of staring at the alien. Either this is because they are Romans, and strangers are negligible, or because foreign visitors arrive in such numbers that they have become an integral part of the city's life. Whatever the reason, it is comforting.

We foreigners are, I suppose, of value to the Romans on account of the money that we bring with us; but there is no visible sign in the streets that we are wanted. No Roman gives us any pavement.

If you turn up the street by the popular Caffè Nazionale —the Via delle Convertite—you will come to the Piazza

S. Silvestro and the General Post Office. It is always well to know where the General Post Office is, even although it does not, as this one does, occupy a site on which once stood a Temple of the Sun. It is well in Rome also to know of the Piazza di S. Silvestro, because the trams start here for the hilly Ludovisi quarter. Trams in transit in foreign cities are so perplexing that it is a great comfort to know where they start. And in Rome, which is one of the most exhausting of all foreign cities, even an athlete may sometimes sink into a tram with a sigh of satisfaction.

S. Silvestro is one of the friendliest of Rome's churches, with its pretty green courtyard and, on the walls, relics of early Christians from the catacombs. You will find many of these tablets in their original position when you go to the Catacombs themselves, but the inscriptions here may be taken as a preparation for the Appian Way excursion.

The church was built and the tablets brought hither by Paul I in the eighth century, after the Longobards had ravaged Rome. Innocent III rebuilt it early in the thirteenth century, and as it was the shrine of the head of John the Baptist he altered the name to S. Silvestro in Capite. Other restorations were made later and the church is now a favourite resort of foreign Catholics in Rome, the pulpit being the gift of an English lady in 1900. I know of no other church with, in proportion to its size, so many votive offerings. St. Anthony's shrine at Padua itself is hardly more popular.

Returning to the Corso we come very soon, on the right, to the Piazza dela Colonna, the column in the centre of which was raised in honour of the Stoic Emperor Marcus Aurelius Antoninus (A.D. 121-180) and of his victories over the Quadi and Marcomanni. The reliefs which coil round the shaft celebrate this triumph. Marcus Aurelius never gave countenance to the Christians, although during his reign they were not harried. None the less, the miracle of the Thundering Legion, which you will see illustrated in bronze on the column, was claimed by the Christians as the result of their prayers. This miracle, which occurred in the campaign against the Quadi in 174 and led to the rout of the enemy, was the sudden outburst of a storm, which simultaneously restored the parched Romans with its rain and confounded the foe with its lightning. A great statue of Marcus Aurelius stood for centuries on the top of the column, but in 1589 Pope Sixtus V substituted the present image of St. Paul, the sculptor of which was Torrigiani, who broke Michael Angelo's nose.

The church on the left of the Corso, opposite the Piazza Colonna, is S. Maria in Via, built over the well on whose surface a picture of the Madonna was found floating. The next church on the left, in a little recess, is S. Marcello al Corso, St. Marcellus being Pope in 308-9. His body is under the high altar. This church, with its florid façade and grandiose statues, can be one of the most brilliantly lighted in all Rome at festival times. Thousands of what appear to be candle flames, but are really little electric bulbs, make it a kind of fairy palace.

On the right is S. Maria in Via Lata, the crypt of which is claimed to be St. Paul's residence as a prisoner in Rome for two years, chained to a gaoler, but allowed to write his epistles and see his friends. Historians are doubtful as to this story, but I must say that the disposition of the crypt as one sees it to-day, and the convincing words of the sacristan, make a very good case. St. Paul, provided that the building is sufficiently old, might well have been housed here; it is perfectly conceivable. But no one will ever make me believe that he and St. Peter, or

THE FONTANA DI TREVI

[*See page* 30

strikes the eye as an artistic intruder, cutting the sombre city in two, as it does, with such a mass of assertive whiteness. But I heard it defended, and very eloquently, for this very quality of colour, because, as its champion said, it shows us what all Rome must have been like in its glory, before the marble was stripped from the walls. For the dingy Colosseum, I suppose, shone once like a lovely symmetrical iceberg; and until the Forum Romanorum and the Palatine palaces were turned into quarry for the rebuilders they must have shone too.

To my mind, the chief fault of the Vittorio Emmanuele memorial is that it is out of scale. To be huge is not necessarily to be more noticeable; size, as size, does not inevitably excite reverence or awe. A less imposing monument might have had more beauty. On the other hand, however, it is a satisfaction to know that the old Roman ambition to build big and magnificently is not wholly extinct. The Vittorio Emmanuele monument has proved that, just as the Palace of Justice, which is also out of scale, proved it a few years earlier.

The golden king on his golden horse, the golden groups, and the golden angels on their pinnacles, add splendour to the whiteness. The King is commanding from every point, but you might remember that a very interesting glimpse of him, quite isolated, is obtained at No. 29 Foro Trajano. It is needless to say that, in order to build the Memorial, a great deal of ground had to be cleared, and many landmarks went. The only ancient relic that is preserved is a fragment, by the fountain on the left, of the tomb of Caius Publicius Bibulus.

Since, not only in Rome, but all over Italy, the name of Vittorio Emmanuele II is continually found, let me say a few words here as to his reign. His special distinction is that he was the first King of Italy. When he came to the throne of Piedmont in 1849, Italy was a country of small states, Austria was a venomous enemy, Rome was full of republicanism, and France and Spain were both on the warpath, with Prussia, never very trustworthy, in the offing. By 1871 Italy was one. It would be idle to pretend that Vittorio Emmanuele could have achieved this end single-handed. Without the political sagacity of Cavour on the one hand, and the personal magnetic genius and energy of Garibaldi on the other, he might have met only with disaster; for his chief gifts were courage and honesty. But he had the discernment to recognize genuineness and the simplicity to trust it, and his character surrounded him with enthusiasts. He died in 1878.

Say what we will of his Memorial, it was a stroke of genius to place the body of the Unknown Warrior there. He lies on the first platform, beneath the figure of Italy, always guarded, and to this shrine votive wreaths are continually being carried. I have watched more than one procession bearing their tributes up the steps, singing as they went, and it is a very touching sight.

From the highest terrace of the Memorial one has a wide view of Rome; but it was a surprise and shock to me to find that the Corso Umberto I, which runs away due north from the giant golden statue of the King, is not straight. At any rate, you cannot see the Piazza del Popolo from it, although from the Piazza, standing under the obelisk by the spouting lions, you can see the Memorial.

Immediately below, the eye is caught by the loggia of S. Marco's church. St. Peter's does not seem so much bigger than its competitive domes in the city. It is only when you are a long way off—for example, on one of the balconies of the Villa d'Este at Tivoli, twenty miles away, that you realize how lofty St. Peter's is; because then that is all of Rome that is visible. Even the heights of

PIAZZA DEL POPOLO AND THE CORSO

the Pincio or Celio do not exist; Rome is just this one solitary eminence rising from the plain.

From the sides of the Memorial you have glimpses of the southern parts of the city. The leaning tower of Nero—the Torre delle Milizie, which tradition makes the altitude from which the Emperor, fiddling, watched Rome burn—is close by in the west; in the south-west, cutting the sky, are the backs of the grand sculptured saints on the coping of S. Giovanni in Laterano. The Forum is a good deal hidden by the buildings on the Capitoline hill.

Having seen the King's magnificent memorial, let us see his simple tomb. It is in the Pantheon, the only perfect pagan building which still stands in Rome. The preservation of the Pantheon is indeed marvellous, when we remember that the centre of the roof has always been open. The first temple on this site was built in 27 B.C. in honour of the gods of the seven planets—Apollo, Diana, Mercury, Venus, Mars, Jupiter and Saturn—and you may see inside it the seven niches in which statues of these deities were placed for worship.

The present temple was built by Hadrian in the second century A.D., the walls and the dome being exactly as he decreed them; and the dome with its diminishing squares is surely one of the most satisfying pieces of architecture in the world. In A.D. 609 Pope Boniface IV transformed the temple into the Christian church of Sancta Maria ad Martyres and consecrated it. Twenty-eight waggon-loads of the bones of martyrs from the catacombs were brought hither and re-interred.

The Pantheon is now the burial place of the Kings of Italy. The severely simple tombs of Vittorio Emmanuele II and Umberto I are here, with constantly renewed tributary wreaths, and books always open for loyal signatures.

Here also lies Raphael.

Chapter V

Towards St. Peter's

The Smallness of Rome—A City of Churches—The Vastness of the Vatican—The St. Peter's habit—St. Peter and Rome—Hagiographers in Conflict—St. Paul and Rome—The Swiss Guard—The Piazza of St. Peter's—Bernini's Colonnades—The Façade of St. Peter's—The First Church of St. Peter—Bramante and later Architects—Michael Angelo's Dome—Comparative Measurements.

TO the question, Which is the part of Rome that most visitors wish most to see, or wish first to see? the answer probably is, St. Peter's.

This being the case, I should perhaps have placed St. Peter's earlier in this record of perambulations; but so much Roman history is referred to in my notes on the Popes buried there that clarity seemed more likely to be served by postponement.

But for its hills Rome is small enough to be explored on foot. Time is usually against this method; but where time need not be considered, I strongly urge it. Indeed, one of the surprises that Rome has in store for the stranger is, how small it is. Milan with its factories, Naples with its teeming tenements, both seem endless in comparison; and there is no reason why they should not be more vast, except that tradition has made Rome the centre of the universe, and the thought carries with it a suggestion of immensity. But Rome is small; and not only small, but almost provincial too. If the Corso Umberto I is the heart of Rome, and the Caffé Nazionale is the heart of the Corso, then it is provincial indeed. Even

Florence has rival establishments; even Venice, where
energy and revolt are not expected. But Rome may
almost truthfully be said to have but one.

Not only does one quickly realize how small Rome is—
how provincial, if you like—but how single is its life.
There are Government buildings; there are shops; there
are hotels and sight-seers; but the real inner essential
Rome is going on all the while insensitive to them: Rome,
the home of the religion that bears its name; Rome, the
spiritual mother of millions. It is the city of the Church,
and the city of churches; churches that were once pagan
temples and churches being built to-day. How many
there are, I have no idea; but it is difficult, if not impossible, to be in any street and not see one; while priests
and monks and seminarists are everywhere. Barefoot
friars are as common as policemen. And the churches
are not only myriad, but they are used. Half of Rome
seems always to be on its knees.

To return to the smallness of Rome—it is such as to
make walking to most places a pleasant and not fatiguing task, particularly as there is so much to beguile the
eye, no matter where you go. But there are certain parts
of Rome where, when you reach them, the real business
of walking has to begin, and as they are very extensive,
my advice to the visitor is to drive to their gates.

The Forum, for instance, can be explored only on foot,
and the Forum is immense and has a thousand different
levels, some at a high altitude. But the Forum, for all
its size and irregularity, requires, I verily believe, less
pedestrian vigour and endurance than St. Peter's and
the Vatican galleries.

Everything that I have said about Rome being small is
nonsense when you go to St. Peter's. When at last you
reach it—that is to say, when you reach the end of the
colonnade where one alights from whatever vehicle has

carried one thither, in order to enjoy the approach on foot and see the dome gradually dropping behind the façade as you near it (which was the one thing that its designer, Michael Angelo, wished not to happen); after the cab has disgorged you, a long journey on foot must be yours before, having avoided or repulsed the last peddler with his brooches (or even having, to his persistence, or pathos, or both, succumbed), you vanish through the portals of the fane.

St. Peter's is, I fancy, not only the Roman magnet that draws every visitor with most power, but the only one that never fails. We promise ourselves that we will walk through the Forum, that we will see the Colosseum by moonlight, that we will descend into the Catacombs, that we will stand before the Dying Gladiator. And we postpone. But our promise to St. Peter's we keep.

My advice to the stranger is to visit St. Peter's often. He will find it more wonderful every time, and more friendly. The arrogant marble Popes will lose some of their arrogance, and the humaner marble Popes will become more human. Pius VI, his pomp laid aside, for ever supplicating in the crypt, will become a man and a brother. But forgetting the function of the cathedral altogether, could there be a more fascinating place in which merely to walk? And the Church of Rome is so tolerant of walkers. Its own flock when not on their knees (and at the Scala Santa they walk even on them) walk ever; and walking ever, themselves, even during the services, resent not the alien who meanders too. My advice to the reader who finds himself at a loss in Rome on a wet day, is to take a cab to St. Peter's and allow Bramante and Michael Angelo to provide him with shelter and solace. Yes, and perhaps the strains of Corelli and Palestrina may soothe him too.

The history of the St. Peter's that we are now to enter

Photograph by Anderson

MONUMENT TO CARDINAL CRISTOFORO DELLA ROVERE
By MINO DA FIESOLE and ANDREA BREGNO
in the Church of S. Maria del Popolo

[See page 35

POPE INNOCENT X
After the Picture by VELASQUEZ *in the
Doria Gallery*

[*See page* 41

begins with the sixteenth century; it is thus a little, but not much, older than our own St. Paul's, its most distinguished derivative. The first stone was laid in 1506, the architect being Raphael's friend, Bramante. But for many centuries before that there had been a church here, the earliest being built over the reputed site of St. Peter's martyrdom. We shall see as we move about the city various spots which tradition associates with St. Peter in the flesh. We shall be shown his actual home, not long since excavated; we shall be shown his prison; but historians differ as to whether he was ever here at all. There is no absolute proof. Yet his actual presence is by no means impossible, and indeed it may be considered even probable, especially as references to his sojourn here and martyrdom here begin in patristic writings as early as the end of the first century. It is even said that it was in Rome that St. Mark had from St. Peter's lips the recollections of Our Lord which formed the basis of St. Mark's Gospel.

The tradition of the Church, of course, is, that St. Peter founded the church of Antioch in the year 36 or 37 and remained there as bishop for seven years. In 43 he came to Rome and presided over the church as its head until his martyrdom under Nero in 67 or 68.

A branch of the argument that St. Peter was in Rome is that St. Paul was, their names being so often united. And of St. Paul, of course, we know more and are in no doubt. We know that having "appealed to Cæsar" after his examination by Felix, he was brought here by a centurion for his first trial, when, although chained as a captive to a soldier, he was allowed such privileges as to live in his own lodgings, to see friends and even to preach. St. Mark was one of his visitors, and Timothy was constantly with him until he left for Asia.

Under his permission to write, St. Paul composed in

Rome the Epistles to the Ephesians, to the Philippians and to Philemon.

The trial, which had been postponed, came on at the close of the year 61, and Paul was acquitted. There then followed four years of travel and propaganda, of which we know very little, and then in the year 65 he was a prisoner in Rome again, this time much more rigorously treated, although not prevented from writing the Second Epistle to Timothy, which some think his best work.

St. Paul's execution, by beheading, is supposed by some authorities to have been in the year 62; Ramsay gives 65. Tertullian, writing in the second century, named the exact spot on the Ostian Way, close to the church of S. Paolo fuori le Mura, where the sword fell. But of this more later.

Advancing towards the Piazza of St. Peter's you will have on your right the great and uncomely bulk of the Papal apartments, rising hugely above the colonnade. That is the Vatican, in which the Pope lives, in which the Sacred College meets, in which are Raphael's frescoes and the galleries of sculpture, and from which you gain the Sistine Chapel to see Michael Angelo's ceiling and Last Judgment. Such a mixture of magnificence and domesticity is it that on the roof you will probably catch sight of washing. The chief entrance to the Vatican is under the colonnade to the right, where the Pope's Swiss Guards stand. Two or three are always looking out of a window here. The Popes, as we shall have reason to know, once had immense armies. To-day they have only a body-guard of Roman noblemen; the Guardia Palatina, a band of fifty Roman gentlemen; and the Swiss Guard, a hundred halberdiers.

The obelisk in the centre of the Piazza where we are now standing was brought to Rome by the Emperor Caligula (A.D. 37-41), and set up in the circus which he constructed round and about this spot. It is the only obelisk in Rome that has no hieroglyphics on it. When moved to its present position, in 1586, it was moved intact. In the museum of St. Peter's, at the end of the left colonnade, are models showing how the transport and erection were effected. Around the obelisk are tablets in the pavement indicating the points of the compass and also the divisions of the Zodiac.

We will now consider the glorious colonnades spreading away from the sides of the cathedral façade, with four rows of columns in each, and each column five yards in circumference. This splendid creation, the work of Bernini, was being carried out in 1655-1667, while England was getting rid of Puritanism and welcoming Charles II. I have said that there are four rows of these pillars in each colonnade; but if you stand on a little round plain stone, of which there are two, one between the obelisk and the fountain on either side, you will find that these four melt into one and the colonnade is composed of single pillars. I think the ends, or openings, of Bernini's colonnade, at the extremity of each arc, are among Rome's noblest architectural inspirations.

I have not counted the Saints and Fathers who strike exemplary attitudes along the colonnade on each side, but there must be hundreds. Rome, on its secular buildings as well as religious, is partial to these guardians of the roof, who look over the city from the copings in every street.

We may now turn our attention to St. Peter's itself, which rises at the head of steps guarded by St. Peter and St. Paul, but is from its Piazza commanding rather than beautiful. We are too near. We want to see it from a distance, from the hills around Rome, from the Capitol, from the Castel Sant' Angelo, from the Pincio, from the Janiculum, along the streets, even through the keyhole

of the gate of the Knights of Malta's garden. There is
a very remarkable view of it from the Lungo Tevere, at
the end of the bridge of Umberto I, where it is absolutely
symmetrical, with the light showing through the cupolas
at each side. Every time that you catch any of these
distant glimpses of it, St. Peter's will be more imposing
and memorable.

The first St. Peter's, built here in memory of St. Peter's
martyrdom, was consecrated in the year 326. The actual
sponsor of the new building which developed into the sublime St. Peter's as we now see it, was Pope Nicholas V,
who in 1452 began the tribune; but fifty years passed before the real task was undertaken, under Pope Julius II,
who designed to lie there when he was dead, but as it
happens did not. It is significant of the splendid ambi-
tions and autocracies of the Popes of the Middle Ages,
and of the Renaissance, of which we are to see so much,
that this supreme building was principally to exist as the
tomb of a single pontiff.

Lazzari Bramante, Donato d'Agnolo, who had been a
painting pupil of Fra Bartolommeo, was in 1506 a man
of sixty. He died in 1514, having made much progress
with the building, towards the end being assisted by
Raphael. The two Sangallos and Peruzzi continued the
operations, and then in 1547 came Michael Angelo, to
add the dome. Michael Angelo died in 1564 before it
could be completed, but left very full plans for Giacomo
della Porta to carry out. The façade, which Michael
Angelo would never have tolerated, was added by Maderna
in 1612, and Bernini put the finishing touches. Among
these was a campanile which quickly had to be pulled down
again. The day of consecration was November 18, 1626,
under Pope Urban VIII.

It should be borne in mind that although Bramante was
followed by other hands, all no doubt not unwilling to

TOWARDS ST. PETER'S

chop and change, the main structure of St. Peter's is his, and it was upon this structure that Michael Angelo set his incomparable dome. Brunelleschi, the architect of the Duomo at Florence, had shown the way; but it was Michael Angelo, adapting Bramante (whose dome was to have been shallower, like that of the Pantheon), who created the magical, now solid, now aerial, thing which stands, and for long has stood, as the symbol of Rome.

A few figures may be given: St. Peter's covers 18,000 square yards; St. Paul's in London 9,400. The height of St. Peter's, from pavement to cross, is 435 feet; St. Paul's is 365. The cupola of St. Peter's, if removed and set up again on the ground, would make a very tolerable little cathedral all by itself.

CHAPTER VI

St. Peter's and Its Tombs: I—Right Aisle

The Porta Santa—Sumptuous Ceremonial—The Bronze Toe—First Impressions of the Interior of St. Peter's—Michael Angelo's Pietà—Macaulay and the Papacy—Leo XII—Paintings in St. Peter's—Sixtus IV—Gregory XIII—The four Piers and their Saints—Gregory XVI—Benedict XIV—Clement XIII and Canova's Tomb—Clement X—Urban VIII—The Barberini Family—Paul III.

HAVING passed within the portico (which you are at liberty not to admire) look back on the entrance wall for the "Navicella," Giotto's famous mosaic known by this name, depicting St. Peter's disastrous attempt to walk on the sea. It is over the central opening and opposite the bronze doors, and therefore, being against the light, not easy to study. I have always thought it impartial and human of the authorities to lay such emphasis, here, on the Apostle's weakness. Inside the church we shall find the incident recorded again, as an altar-piece.

The door on the extreme right is the Porta Santa, which is opened only in Holy Year. It was formally closed by the Pope on December 24, 1925, as these eyes can testify, and will not be opened again until December 24, 1949.

All strangers in Rome, when the opportunity arises of seeing a great festival of the Church, should seize it; for there is nothing like it anywhere else. On this occasion, the most precious relics are exhibited (at the gallery altar, high on the S. Veronica pier); but it is the procession, heralded by the papal march played on the silver trumpets, that one remembers most vividly.

54

ST. PETER'S AND ITS TOMBS

The members of the Pope's bodyguard of gentlemen, moving about the church in their capacity as ushers, are mediæval enough, in their ruffs and capes and knee-breeches, with dazzling sword hilts; but clothes are mere accessories, whereas faces are facts, and the true Middle Ages arrive with the procession itself and the countenances of the princes, prelates, priests and monks of the Church. For these faces do not change. There is not one, among all the sumptuously attired company, that one has not seen before, in this picture or that, Ghirlandaio's famous kind old bottle-nosed priest in the Louvre alone being absent.

Some of the clerics are in purple, some in black, some in cowls; one or two are bearded; some austerely robed in white, with a cabalistic design. Many are incredibly old; almost none look happy, care-free; many are lined and marked by anxiety. And then the cardinals, in their crimson splendour, bringing with them murmurs and scents of the infinite Dumas; and then, carried high above all the rest, by servitors in red, and accompanied by two bearers of lofty feather fans, the Holy Father himself, seated in his chair, with a great yellow mitre on his venerable head, and softly waving his hand from right to left in blessing.

Nothing in the great cathedral seems to change except that St. Peter's right foot is always being kissed into greater deformity. Although made of endurable bronze, the toes have not endured. This strikes me as a great mystery, because if one were to take a photograph of the foot after every kiss and the kisses are not such passionate affairs either—it is probable that no difference would be distinguishable; and yet the detrition is going on all the time. This figure of St. Peter, by the way, which is to be found at the end of the right wall of the nave, close to the baldacchino, is nearer life-size than almost anything in the cathedral, where a gigantic scale has been followed by architects, sculptors and painters alike. The Founders of the Spiritual Orders set in niches in the nave and the transepts are giants. Ignatius Loyola, for example, on the wall opposite St. Peter, declaiming from a book while Satan writhes in failure at his feet, is a colossus. The cherubim who, on the walls, in pairs, display medallions of the Popes, are little mammoths; the doves with the olive branch in their beaks, occurring rhythmically among these cherubs, are as big as turkeys. Oversize is the note—vastness—and vastness made more vast by the emptiness of the floor, which, except on special occasions, has no chairs. It is when the rich red hangings cover the white marble and the gold that St. Peter's condescends a little. Vastness, emptiness, these may be the first impressions; but amid them you are conscious of the golden lambency diffused by the Holy Spirit at the far, far end. Whatever the weather or the time of day, this symbol has its own effulgence.

But if the vastness and coolness repel rather than allure, if St. Peter's is more suggestive of strength than sweetness, there are still two refuges for the chilled or frightened visitant. In the first chapel on the right as he enters he will find that most tender and beautiful and pathetic group, the Pietà of Michael Angelo, which seems always to grow in beauty and tenderness and pathos, and which is more easily seen than that other Pietà from the same hand, his last work—as this is almost his earliest—in the Duomo at Florence. And just to the left as you enter, beyond the Baptistery, you will find the Jacobite monument by Canova, with the lovely mourning figures beneath the medallion of the fated Stuarts.

I should like here to quote the account of the Pietà given by Michael Angelo's friend and biographer, Vasari: "To this work let no sculptor, however rare a craftsman,

THE PANTHEON

[*See page* 31

ever think to be able to approach in design or in grace,
or ever to be able, with all the pains in the world, to attain
to such delicacy and smoothness or to perforate the
marble with such art as Michelagnolo did therein, for in
it may be seen all the power and worth of art. Among the
lovely things to be seen in the work, to say nothing of the
divinely beautiful draperies, is the body of Christ; nor
let any one think to see greater beauty of members or
more mastery of art in any body, or a nude with more
detail in muscles, veins and nerves over the framework of
the bones, nor yet a corpse more similar than this to a real
corpse. Here is perfect sweetness in the expression of the
head, harmony in the joints and attachments of the arms,
legs, and trunk, and the pulses and veins so wrought, that
in truth Wonder herself must marvel that the hand of a
craftsman should have been able to execute so divinely
and so perfectly, in so short a time, a work so admirable;
and it is certainly a miracle that a stone without any
shape at the beginning should ever have been reduced to
such perfection as Nature is scarcely able to create in
the flesh.

"Such were Michelagnolo's love and zeal together in
this work, that he left his name—a thing that he never
did again in any other work—written across a girdle that
encircles the bosom of Our Lady. And the reason was
that one day Michelagnolo, entering the place where it
was set up, found there a great number of strangers from
Lombardy, who were praising it highly, and one of them
asked one of the others who had done it, and he answered,
'Our Gobbo, from Milan.' Michelagnolo stood silent, but
thought it something strange that his labours should be
attributed to another; and one night he shut himself in
there, and having brought a little light and his chisels,
carved his name upon it.

"From this work he acquired very great fame, and

although certain persons, rather fools than otherwise, say that he has made Our Lady too young, are these so ignorant as not to know that unspotted virgins maintain and preserve their freshness of countenance a long time without any mark, and that persons afflicted as Christ was do the contrary? That circumstance, therefore, won an even greater increase of glory and fame for his genius than all his previous works."

Let us make a tour of the floor, beginning with the Michael Angelo chapel in the right aisle. Next to this is the monument to Leo XII (1823-1829), and opposite that, the monument to Maria Christina of Sweden, daughter of Gustavus Adolphus, and a convert to Rome.

Where only the monument exists, I should say, the actual tomb, simple and severe, is in the grotto beneath the floor of the transepts. Most of the monuments are, however, also the actual tombs.

Before we examine the tomb of the first of the long line of Popes, all of whom are in some way or another commemorated here, let me borrow from Macaulay's essay on Von Ranke's history a melodious passage that shall serve as an overture or introduction: "There is not, and there never was on this earth, a work of human policy so well deserving of examination as the Roman Catholic Church. The history of that Church joins together the two great ages of human civilization. No other institution is left standing which carries the mind back to the times when the smoke of sacrifice rose from the Pantheon, and when camelopards and tigers abounded in the Flavian amphitheatre. The proudest royal houses are but of yesterday when compared with the line of Supreme Pontiffs. That line we trace back in an unbroken series, from the Pope who crowned Napoleon in the nineteenth century to the Pope who crowned Pepin in the eighth; and far beyond the time of Pepin the august dynasty extends, till it is lost in the twilight of fable. The republic of Venice came next in antiquity. But the republic of Venice was modern when compared with the Papacy; and the republic of Venice is gone, and the Papacy remains. The Papacy remains, not in decay, not a mere antique, but full of life and youthful vigour. The Catholic Church is still sending forth to the farthest ends of the world missionaries as zealous as those who landed in Kent with Augustine, and still confronting hostile kings with the same spirit with which she confronted Attila. The number of her children is greater than in any former age. Her acquisitions in the New World have more than compensated for what she has lost in the Old. Her spiritual ascendancy extends over the vast countries which lie between the plains of the Missouri and Cape Horn, countries which, a century hence, may not improbably contain a population as large as that which now inhabits Europe. The members of her communion are certainly not fewer than a hundred and fifty millions; and it will be difficult to show that all other Christian sects united amount to a hundred and twenty millions. Nor do we see any sign which indicates that the term of her long dominion is approaching. She saw the commencement of all the governments and of all the ecclesiastical establishments that now exist in the world; and we feel no assurance that she is not destined to see the end of them all. She was great and respected before the Saxon had set foot on Britain, before the Frank had passed the Rhine, when Grecian eloquence still flourished in Antioch, when idols were still worshipped in the temple of Mecca. And she may still exist in undiminished vigour when some traveller from New Zealand shall, in the midst of a vast solitude, take his stand on a broken arch of London Bridge to sketch the ruins of St. Paul's."

Leo XII, before whose monument we are now standing, succeeded Pius VII, the Pope whose reign had covered the period of Napoleon's rise and fall, and who, with the Church, had suffered at his hands. Collectors of co-incidences may be interested in reading that Leo came to the throne a sick man and in 1824 was given up by the physicians, but on Bishop Strambi of Macerata offering his life in his stead, began to rally. The Bishop it was that died: the Pope survived until 1829.

We come now to the first altar-piece—and here let me say that many of St. Peter's altar-pieces are mosaic copies, the originals having been removed—and none are very remarkable. The best pictures are in the Pontifical Gallery, which we shall soon visit; St. Peter's is for sculpture and architecture. This altar-piece, the Martyrdom of St. Sebastian, is a copy of the original by Domenichino now in Santa Maria degli Angeli. In the right niche of the arch that we now pass through is the tomb of Innocent XII. His reign (1691-1700) was not epoch-making, but in person he was beloved for his benevolence to the poor and afflicted, as the sculptor means to suggest by the figure of Charity at the left and of Justice at the right, both very happy creations.

Opposite the tomb of Innocent XII is a monument to the Countess Matilda of Tuscia by Bernini. The large chapel where suppliants kneel at the gates, is that of the Holy Sacrament. It was in this chapel that Pope Sixtus IV (1471-1484) had his tomb of bronze; but in 1925 it was moved to the Museum of St. Peter's, just off the Piazza. Let me, however, assume that it is still in its old place, and say something of this pontiff, who exercised a determined will in turbulent times and left an indelible mark on Rome—Francesco della Rovere, known as Sixtus IV, and the uncle of Julius II. A large part of his reign was occupied in a feud with the Medici, which led to civil war here and there in Italy, until the invasion of Sicily

ST. PETER'S AND ITS TOMBS

by the Turks united these brotherly foes. The story belongs perhaps more to Florence than Rome.

Sixtus IV built the Sixtine, or Sistine, Chapel, which we are soon to see, and to Rome from his hated Tuscany brought Botticelli, Luca Signorelli, Perugino and other famous artists to beautify it. Later Michael Angelo added the ceiling under Julius II. Sixtus also gave Rome its Ponte Sisto. His superb bronze tomb by Antonio del Pollaiuolo we shall see in the Museum; while in the Vatican Picture Gallery is Melozzo da Forli's fresco of the Pope, with Julius II, then a Cardinal, kneeling to him.

In the next arch, on the right, is the tomb of Gregory XIII (1572-1585), bearded and authoritative, from a design by Michael Angelo. This was the Pope Gregory who gave his name to the Gregorian Calendar. During his reign occurred the Massacre of St. Bartholomew, in honour of which he ordered a medal to be struck. The Quirinale, now the palace of the King, but for centuries one of the palaces of the Popes, was built by him.

Next, on the left, is the tomb of Gregory XIV (1590-1591) without any statue. This Pope, who came to the throne in 1590 and reigned only ten months, was chiefly occupied in enforcing the excommunication of Henry of Navarre, who, however, two years afterwards, solved many problems by becoming a Catholic.

Here we turn to the right, the altar-piece opposite being another copy of Domenichino, the Communion of St. Jerome. The turn to the right is caused by the great pier, against which is the Domenichino altar-piece. These piers are four in number and are allotted to St. Longinus (this one), St. Helena, St. Veronica and St. Andrew. It will be remembered that St. Andrew was also crucified, St. Longinus was the Roman soldier who mercifully pierced the side of the dying Christ, St. Helena afterwards found the Cross and brought it back to Jerusa-

61

lem, and St. Veronica lent the Saviour her handkerchief, on which the imprint of His features remained. This handkerchief, St. Longinus's spear, either the head of St. Andrew or a piece of his cross and a portion of the true Cross are kept in reliquaries and displayed on special occasions.

Resuming our perambulation of the right aisle, we find on the right the tomb of Gregory XVI, who came to the throne in 1831 and died in 1846, and who was so reactionary as to forbid the construction of railways in the Papal States, and in many other ways to wield Mrs. Partington's mop. Under him the Church of Rome, already crippled, lost much of its power. I find in a pleasant book of travel now out of print entitled *Art and Nature under an Italian Sky*, by M. J. M. D., an English lady, first published in 1852, an interesting account of an interview with this Pope, which has a reference to his dislike of the Iron Horse:

"We were directed to courtesy three times as we advanced, which we did with all due solemnity. He received us very kindly, and, as it was a private reception, with little of form or ceremony. We were told he rather enjoyed seeing English ladies in this quiet way, especially if they are introduced by any of his personal friends. Our names being repeated, we advanced near him, and he addressed us individually. He never speaks but in Italian, so that it was rather awful, considering my but recent renewal of acquaintance with that language to be obliged to answer his queries. Fortunately, he took most of the conversation upon himself. He asked me, however, what I thought of Rome, of St. Peter's, and of the Miserere, which had been performed the previous day; questioned me of my home; how we had performed the journey from England, and such like. I named the railway among other modes of travelling, and was glad I had done so, as it

called forth the most characteristic expression of opinion
with which we were favoured. In the most energetic manner he declared his dislike of railways; adding, that
though he doubted not when he was 'sotto terra' railways would speedily be introduced into the Papal States,
yet that as long as he lived not one should be permitted.

" . . . We were told rather an interesting anecdote
concerning this Pontiff, which I have good reason to
believe true. A lady, more full of zeal than discretion,
left England and went to Rome, with one fixed object
in view,—the conversion of the Pope. She sought and
obtained an interview with him, and, by way of over-
whelming him at once, put before him the infinite pre-
sumption of which he must be guilty in setting himself
up as the infallible teacher of Christendom. He listened
to her calmly for some time, and then said, 'I thank you,
madam, for your zeal on my behalf. Believe me, not a
day of my life passes that I do not humble myself before
my God, feeling and knowing myself to be a sinner, and
asking forgiveness. But having said this, allow me to ask
you if your own spirit is a right one, and if the mission
you have now undertaken shows *yourself* to be possessed
of that true humility, which, as you have well said, must
be the foundation of Christianity.' It is not difficult to
believe what was added,—that the romantic lady was
so melted by the meekness and forbearance of His
Holiness, that she herself became a decided convert to
Popery!"

The next altar has, set in the midst of precious marbles,
the representation of the Madonna del Soccorso, from the
old church of St. Peter, one of Rome's tutelary saints.
The early Father, St. Gregory Nazianzen, who died in
the fourth century, is buried beneath this altar.

The next tomb on the right is that of Benedict XIV
(1740-1758), and in its florid way it is, I think, one of the

best. The pontiff so gaily commemorated by the sculptor
was a Bolognese, a scholar, author and wit, but he was
so severe upon certain laxities in the Church that he was
called the "Protestant Pope." He was sufficiently a
Jacobite to have a medal struck in memory of Maria
Sobieski, the wife of the Old Pretender, calling her
"Queen of Britain."

We now reach the right transept, at the end of which
are three altars with very dark paintings, the third being
after Nicholas Poussin, the great French painter who
settled in Rome in 1643 and died there. Re-entering the
right aisle, we come, on the right, to the papal monument
which many critics think the finest of all—that of Clement
XIII by Canova. Of Canova I shall say something later;
here merely remarking that, both he and the Pope being
Venetians, there was peculiar reason for the choice of
the sculptor and for the Venetian symbolism on the tomb.
Clement XIII (1758-1769) who was a Jesuit and a member of the Rezzonico family, from which Doges had
sprung, had a chequered career as Pope, owing to the
hostility of the Catholic Powers to the Jesuits, which,
presuming on his gentleness, burst out in Europe. The
Pope resisted all demands for the suppression of the
Order, although his successor, Clement XIV, had to concede it. Clement XIV is not buried here but at the
Church of the Apostles, his tomb also being by Canova.

The altar-piece opposite, against the wall of St.
Helena's pier, again depicts St. Peter walking on the
water.

The last section of the right aisle is called the Chapel
of the Archangel Michael, the altar-piece being after
Guido Reni. Under the arch we find on the right the
monument to Clement X (1670-1676), and on the left
an altar-piece of St. Peter raising Tabitha. Clement X,
whose tomb has some charming touches, was one of the

PIETÀ
After the Statue by MICHAEL ANGELO *in*
St. Peter's

[*See page* 56

IACOBO·III
IACOBI·II·MAGNAE·BRIT·REGIS·FILIO
KAROLO·EDVARDO
ET·HENRICO·DECANO·PATRVM·CARDINALIVM
IACOBI·III·FILIIS
REGIAE·STIRPIS·STVARDIAE·POSTREMIS
ANNO·M·DCCC·XIX

Photograph by Anderson

THE STUART MONUMENT
    By CANOVA *in St. Peter's*

[*See page* 72

ST. PETER'S AND ITS TOMBS

Altieri family of Rome. Coming to the throne in his eightieth year, he exercised no great personal power. The angels by Bernini on the Ponte Sant' Angelo were commissioned by him, and the two fountains which we saw in the Piazza of St. Peter's he also decreed.

Enclosed in the bronze gallery above the tribune altar is the actual ivory throne on which St. Peter is said to have sat.

Two Popes lie in the tribune choir—on the right Urban VIII and on the left Paul III. Urban VIII (1623-1644), a member of the Barberini family, although a poet and friend of learning, was sufficiently afraid of enlightenment to support the Inquisition in its treatment of Galileo. His statecraft was not conspicuous, but he did what he could to make Rome more beautiful, even though, in the task, he destroyed much that was old and precious. When the great French landscape painter, Claude, came to Rome, Urban VIII was his first patron. It was he who commissioned the colonnade of St. Peter's, while to the church itself he gave the baldacchino over the high altar, also the work of Bernini. The Barberini bees, which you will find in the bronze, are indeed everywhere in Rome, and of course at the Barberini Palace, another of Bernini's efforts for this Pope.

Paul III (1534-1549), whose tomb is opposite that of Urban VIII, was also of noble family—one of the Farnese of Rome—and it was he who began the Farnese Palace, which is still one of the most magnificent of Roman Renaissance buildings. His reign was troubled by disorders within the Church, the Counter-Reformation being then in progress, with Henry VIII a sharp thorn in Rome's side. Paul III was painted both by Raphael and Titian. The famous portrait of the old man with his long beard and thin features (like a ghost), with his two grandsons beside him, is one of the glories of the Naples Museum.

CHAPTER VII

St. Peter's and Its Tombs: II—Left Aisle

Leo the Great and other Leonine Popes—Alexander VII—Confession in seven Tongues—A Roman Dwarf—Giotto in Rome—From Circus to Sacristy—St. Gregory the Great and the English Youths—St. Augustine—Pius VII and Napoleon—Innocent VIII—The Old Pretender—Bonnie Prince Charlie—A King in Exile—Canova—Pius VI and his Statue in the Confessio—Pius IX—S. Lorenzo fuori le Mura—Evangelists in Mosaic—The Museum of St. Peter's—Models and Plans.

WE now proceed on our way to the left aisle, through an arch which on the right has the tomb of Alexander VIII, and, opposite, an altar-piece, against the St. Veronica pier, representing St. Peter and St. John healing the Lame Man. Alexander VIII (1689-1691), who was of the Venetian family of Ottoboni, came to the throne in his eightieth year and made little mark.

In the chapel of the Colonna are altars dedicated to four early Popes—on the right, St. Leo the First, and on the left, St. Leo II, St. Leo III and St. Leo IV. St. Leo I, one of the wisest and most powerful of the Popes, known as the Great, reigned for twenty-one years from 440 to 461. He had peculiar difficulties to contend against both within and without the Church. The Manicheans, who denied the Incarnation of Christ, had to be suppressed, and then Eutyches, who supported the Nestorian heresy that the title "Mother of God" could not be given to the Virgin Mary. The Roman Emperor, Valentinian III, was also a problem on account of his turpitude, and such was his cowardice that when the terrible Attila fell upon Rome and the Emperor had fled, it was the Pope

66

who had to confront the Hun in person and arrange a peace.

The next altar contains the remains of three other Leonine Popes, also Saints: St. Leo II (682-683), St. Leo III (795-816) and St. Leo IV (847-855). Of St. Leo II there is little to tell. The sanctity of St. Leo III is not accepted by all historians. His reign was marked by disturbances in Rome, in one of which he was taken prisoner and maltreated; he also had acrimonious passages with Charlemagne. St. Leo IV was the builder of what is known as the Leonine Wall round the Vatican Hill. When Alfred the Great, at the age of five, was sent to Rome to be blessed, this was the Pope who blessed him. If ever there was a Pope Joan—as legendary lore likes to believe—it was after the death of Leo IV that she ruled.

We now proceed rapidly from the ninth to the seventeenth century, the next monument, on the right, being that to Alexander VII (1655-1667), one of the family of Chigi, of Siena, an earlier scion of which had been Agostino Chigi, the banker and Raphael's patron. Alexander's reign was not brilliant, as he embroiled the Papal States with France and preferred scholarly and poetical pursuits to administration. The tomb is by Bernini.

We now enter the left transept, where there are three altars, and confessional boxes for seven tongues. None of the altars, however, has a picture of the Building of Babel. The tomb in front of the middle altar is that of Giovanni Pier Luigi da Palestrina (1526-1594), the composer of some of the loveliest church music that we hear in this city. The pictures are too dark to be studied.

We come now to the entrance to the Sacristy, over which is the monument to Pius VIII (1829-1830), who, in poor health throughout his brief reign, had few chances to impress himself.

A WANDERER IN ROME

On my way to the Sacristy on a recent visit I met the smallest woman I have ever seen, free. She was very old and wrinkled and dressed entirely in black, and I doubt if she could have measured more than three feet six inches. Rome has many dwarfs, but this was the champion. By an odd chance the church was that day being inspected by a music-hall giant, with a retinue of gapers. He crossed the Piazza in a tall hat of pantomime dimensions, looking, as he entered the atrium, almost life-size. But St. Peter then took him in hand and diminished him.

An attendant will lead you to the inner room where the Giottos are. These, which are among the earliest conscious works of art in paint, are interesting not only for their age, but because they would still be very delightful if done yesterday, grim though their subjects be. One represents the martyrdom of St. Peter, being crucified head downwards, and one the decapitation of St. Paul. Giotto has so composed and painted that one loses sight of the tragedy and thinks only of the artist's charm. The colours are still gay. This early artist, who was born in 1267, was in Rome in 1298, making for St. Peter's the mosaic of the "Navicella" and these pictures, and, a little later, for the Lateran, the fresco of Boniface VIII which we are to see. But for Giotto's best work Assisi and Padua must, of course, be visited.

Standing in the Sacristy we are on the very centre of the site of Caligula's circus, where Christians were torn to pieces by lions, and even burned as human torches, for Nero's gratification.

We now recede into early papel history again, the tomb before us on the right, in the chapel of St. Clement, being that of St. Gregory the Great (590-604), perhaps the most imposing figure in the whole long line of Popes, and one of peculiar interest to the English because it was he who, as a deacon, visited England with the tidings of

ST. PETER'S AND ITS TOMBS

Christianity. The story is often told that St. Gregory, who was renowned not only for piety and diligence but for his pleasant wit, seeing in the slave market in the Forum some blond youths and asking where they came from, was told that they were Angles. "Not Angles, but Angels," is the ordinary version of his comment. But the conversation, as I find it in Father Chandlery's *Pilgrim Walks in Rome,* is longer.

Thus, on the dealer replying "From Britain," St. Gregory asked if that land was Christian or still in pagan darkness? "Still pagan," said the merchant. "What a pity," said St. Gregory, "that the Author of Darkness should own such fair faces, and with such outward grace of form they should lack inward grace."

On learning that they were Angles, St. Gregory said, "True; they have angelic faces and should be co-heirs with angels in Heaven."

On learning that the name of the province in Britain from which they had come was Deira, St. Gregory said: "Yes; *de ira* : snatched from ire and called to the mercy of Christ."

On learning that the name of their king was Alla, St. Gregory said, "Alleluia! The praise of God must be sung in those parts."

St. Gregory himself was not long in Britain, being called back to become Pope, but afterwards, in 596, he sent St. Augustine (who became the first Archbishop of Canterbury) with his monks, as every schoolboy knows. Some idea of the energy and zeal which St. Gregory displayed in his office may be gained from the vast mass of his correspondence that has been preserved. It was, of course, from him that the Gregorian chant was named.

The saint's remains were moved from time to time, always with extreme reverence, and finally came to rest here in 1606 under Paul V. He has his own church in

69

Rome, S. Gregorio on the Cœlian Hill, in which his cell, moved from his ancient Benedictine monastery of St. Andrew, may be seen. There, also, is a representation of the Pope witnessing the apparition of the Archangel Michael on the summit of the Castel Sant' Angelo.

It is told of this very human Pope that one day, contemplating the ruins of Trajan's Forum and remembering the good acts of that Emperor, he interceded in prayer with the Almighty and obtained the release of Trajan's soul from Purgatory.

The next papal tomb, close by, is that of Pius VII, who came to the throne as recently as the year 1800, and, living till 1823, thus had the misfortune to coincide with Napoleon, who treated him with little respect. Napoleon, in fact, wished to be Pope as well as Emperor. From 1808 until 1814 Pius VII was a prisoner in France. After Waterloo a certain amount of political re-adjustment occurred, but the Church of Rome was never again so powerful as it had been before Austerlitz. As for Napoleon's loot from Rome, much of that will probably never be restored. This tomb is by Thorwaldsen, the Danish sculptor.

We come, on the left, against the wall of St. Andrew's pier, to an enlarged copy of Raphael's Transfiguration in mosaic, the original being in the Pontifical Gallery near by. This work, made in the Vatican mosaic studios (which may be visited), took ten men nine years to piece together.

In the passage between the Chapel of St. Clement and the Choir are two papal tombs: on the right Leo XI, and on the left Innocent XI. Leo XI was one of the Medici family of Florence, whose principal work had been to restore the Catholic religion to France after Henri IV had entered the Church of Rome. His reign as Pope did not last through the year 1605.

ST. PETER'S AND ITS TOMBS

Innocent XI (1676-1689) was more important, exercising a strong will within the Church, but his ceaseless quarrel with Louis XIV of France and everybody French led to costly strife.

Now comes the beautiful Coro, or chapel of the Choir, where one so often finds a service being celebrated; feasts both for ear and eye. The stalls date from the reign of Urban VIII (1623-1644).

Two other papal monuments remain, confronting each other, one of the fifteenth century in dark bronze and the other of the twentieth in glistening marble: on the left of the passage way after the Choir being the Pollaiuolo brothers' beautiful tomb of Innocent VIII, and, opposite, Pius X, who died in 1914, and whose body is in the Grotto of the church in a plain sarcophagus.

Innocent VIII had an inauspicious reign. It was he who tempted fate (had he known) by making young Giovanni de' Medici a Cardinal at the age of fourteen, for this boy was one day to be Pope Leo X. The head of the spear with which St. Longinus pierced the side of Christ on the Cross came to St. Peter's as a gift from the Turkish Sultan during Innocent VIII's reign.

Pius X (1903-1914) was a gentle creature, greatly beloved.

We now come to an object of poignant historic interest to English and Scottish visitors—Canova's monument to the three luckless Stuarts, which Sir Walter Scott, late in life, journeyed to Rome expressly to see. I have already referred to the beauty of the mourning figures.

The three Stuarts who are commemorated here are James Francis Edward Stuart, the "Old Pretender," his elder son, Charles Edward, or Bonnie Prince Charlie, and his younger son, Henry, Cardinal of York. The "Old Pretender," whose life was one long series of frustrations and even his birth a matter of fraud, was the second

71

son of James II and Mary of Modena, and was nominally born at St. James's Palace in London in 1688, but as a matter of fact was smuggled into his putative mother's bed from without. His early years were spent abroad, and meanwhile William of Orange had become William III of England and sat on the throne with his Queen Mary. On the death of James II in exile in 1701, the boy was acclaimed king by his partisans as James III of England and James VIII of Scotland, but without avail, and in the same year a law was passed to preclude the male line of Stuarts from ever becoming kings of England again. Then began that series of Jacobite plots and campaigns but for which English romantic fiction would be poor indeed.

In 1702 James's half-sister Anne came to the throne, but showed him no friendliness, and in 1714, when the throne was vacant again, the Hanoverians made their appearance. Under the title of the Chevalier, James took some part in fighting with the French. In 1716 he was actually crowned in Scotland, but having neither the personality nor power to inspire his followers to any tremendous effort, he fled before the constitutional army and took refuge on the Continent, where, roving here and there and always intriguing, most of his life was spent.

In 1719 he was married by proxy to the Princess Maria Clementine Sobieski, of the royal Polish line, whose monument is opposite his own. Her he treated badly, and, in consequence, she retired to a nunnery: not, however, before his sons, Charles Edward and Henry, were born.

James was now a resident in Rome, and kept some kind of court there for Jacobites. The last effort to gain his rights was the tragic adventure of the '45, the brunt of which was borne by his elder son. The Old Pretender died in 1766, and with his death came to a close one of the most futile and pathetic careers in his-

THE CORSO UMBERTO I WITH THE VITTORIO EMMANUELE
MONUMENT AT THE SOUTHERN END

[*See page* 38

ST. PETER'S AND ITS TOMBS

tory. Thomas Gray, the poet of the *Elegy*, when travelling in Italy, found in him a likeness to James II, but says he was awkward and ill-made, with a most unpromising countenance, and that he had the look of an idiot, particularly when laughing or praying. "The first he does not often; the latter continually." The Old Pretender lay in state, wearing his crown, for three days, in the Church of the Twelve Apostles. His tomb was paid for by George III.

Charles Edward Stuart, the Young Pretender, who is also buried here, was born in Rome in 1720. Of his life in the years immediately following the débâcle of the '45, little is known, but in 1756 he was living at Basle, and in 1766, after his father's death, when he called himself King of England, he too settled in Rome, and (after a sojourn in Florence with his illegitimate daughter, whom he created Duchess of Albany), died there in 1788.

A word may be said here as to Canova, the sculptor of the Stuart monument, who, although a son of Venetian soil, did much of his work in and for Rome. Antonio Canova, born in 1757, was brought up by his grandparents, who early discerned his ability and fostered it in every way possible. The story goes that the model of a cow in butter which the boy produced (the same medium in which the Prince of Wales was moulded at Wembley) attracted the notice of one of the princely Faliers of Venice, who thereupon became the boy's patron and saw to it that he was properly instructed. Canova reached Rome in 1780 and flung himself into the rapture of studying the sculpture in its galleries and profiting by the lessons conveyed.

His first masterpiece was the tomb of Clement XIV, which we shall see at the Twelve Apostles; his second, the tomb of Clement XIII, which we saw just now in the right aisle of St. Peter's. But the work of Canova which

73

wins the popular vote is the nude recumbent figure of
Napoleon's sister, Pauline, who became the Princess
Borghese, in the Casino of the Villa Umberto I.

Canova's studio was near the Via del Babuino. He died
in 1822, full of honours, and was buried in the Frari in
Venice in the lovely tomb which he had designed for
Titian's second funeral.

The last, or first, chapel in the left aisle of St. Peter's
is the Baptistery. For the ascent to the Dome you apply
at the door under the Sobieski monument; but I advise
you not to adventure on a windy day.

There remain to be mentioned two other Popes commemorated in St. Peter's: Pius VI (1775-1799), whose
kneeling figure by Canova is in the Confessio praying
for ever more; and Pius IX, whose portrait is over
the figure of St. Peter in the nave. Pius VI, who had
no wish to become Pope, began with financial reforms
and did much to enrich the Vatican art galleries; but
the French Revolution sounded his knell and he died a
prisoner, under Napoleon Buonaparte's orders, in Valence,
leaving behind him a despoiled Church and a despoiled
Italy.

Why this Pope should have this unique position in the
Confessio I have not learned. Perhaps because of his
simple piety and in recognition of the unhappiness and
frustration of his reign. His is indeed the place of honour.
Seventy perpetual flames surround him, and immediately
before his eyes is the chapel containing the sarcophagus
of St. Peter himself.

Pius IX was born in 1792 and elected Pope in 1846.
His reign lasted until 1878 and thus coincided with some
of the most turbulent passages in Italian and European
history, which proved too much for his ability to deal
with; and in the end he had to see the loss both of the
Papal States and of the Quirinale, and thus became the

1154) moved it to San Giovanni in Laterano to be his
own tomb, while St. Helena's remains are now at the
Aracœli. The other sarcophagus was made for Constantine the Great's daughter, St. Constantia, whose church
of St. Agnes, built for her by her father, may be visited
outside the Porta Pia. Adjoining it is the little chapel
of St. Constantia, converted from her mausoleum by
Alexander IV (1254–1261). The catacombs of St. Agnes,
who miraculously healed and converted the Emperor's
daughter, are particularly interesting.

This sarcophagus also was the object of papal envy,
Paul II the Venetian (1464–1471) having actually removed it to San Marco just before he died; but Sixtus IV
(1471–1484) had it carried back. It was Pius VI who
established it here in 1788.

Other treasures in this room include a statue of the
Emperor Augustus making a speech, and some very attractive bas-reliefs.

In the next room, built by Pius VI, we find more
mosaics in the centre, with a marvellous porphyry basin
posed upon them, and the famous golden figure of Hercules—really bronze, gilt—dominating all. The theory is
that, having been an object of worship, this statue, when
the Twilight of the Gods set in, was overturned: hence
certain damage. It was found in an underground cell,
as though hidden there by one of the faithful, and bought
by Pius IX. The most superb statue in the room is,
however, that of Antinous, the youth whom the Emperor
Hadrian adored; but where all is so fine it is difficult to
choose. The famous head of the Father of the Gods is
here; and from the busts we are able to form an idea of
what this Emperor and that, who moved about Rome
and helped to make it marvellous, were like.

We come now (I am following the order of the official
catalogue) to the Room of the Nine Muses, who are found

to be more vivacious and modern than one would expect. Thalia, for example, could be made quite of our own day in a few minutes by a coiffeur and modiste. I like a Silenus here, No. 491; and the bearded orator, No. 530, called Lycurgus, is very real.

The Room of the Animals is popular, and justly so, because here the learned and the simple can equally be pleased. For some of us the Greek ideal of perfection of human form may be too lofty, too frigid, too remote from our own experience, but we all are capable, cultured and ignorant alike, of pleasure in the fact that a chisel working on a block of marble has evolved a recognizable greyhound which might, in real life, answer our whistle. I have noted a few numbers: 238 a goat and kid, 194 a sow and litter, 180 a goat, 116, 117, 169 greyhounds, 155 a puma in grey marble, 154 a panther in oriental alabaster with its spots of black and yellow marble, 153 a shepherd among his goats asleep, 115 a bitch with a puppy, and Nos. 232 the Minotaur, and 182 Bottom the Weaver, or words to that effect.

Just as we leave, we find No. 138, a centaur returning from hunting, with Eros riding on his back. He has caught a hare. This group was found under the earth of a garden in the Lateran: a circumstance which again leads to surprise that more amateur excavators do not buy plots of land about Rome for the fun of digging in them. Digging is tedious toil, but any drudgery would be well repaid by the discovery of a centaur.

The Room of the Animals leads to the Gallery of the Statues and Busts, which is a *cul-de-sac*, and you see at once on the left the Sleeping Ariadne, one of its principal glories; but had I the offer I should choose the seated figure of Menander at the other end. The history of the Ariadne is not known, but Julius II brought it to the

ANTINOUS AS BACCHUS
  *After the Statue in the Sala Rotunda
  of the Vatican*

[*See page* 79

MENANDER
  *After the Statue in the Galleria delle
  Statue in the Vatican*

[*See page* 80

Vatican. Many people who have never been to Rome may know it from the bronze replica in the Louvre.

The riches of this gallery are in such profusion that no book would hold their praises. No. 253 a Triton, or sea-centaur; No. 264 Apollo Sauroctonus, after Praxiteles; the drunken Satyr, No. 267; and the Roman and his wife, from a tomb (perhaps Cato and Portia), No. 388, should be looked for. And of course the Menander.

The little Room of the Masks, opposite the door near the Ariadne, has the Satyr in *rosso antico* with the gleaming eyes, whom we shall find again at the Capitoline; the Dancing Girl; and a porphyry chair and vase. The name, the Gabinetto delle Maschere, comes from the mosaic of masks on the floor, brought here from Hadrian's villa at Tivoli. Even the fiercest foe to mosaic must be charmed by the delicacy of these pictures.

The catalogue now takes us to the Octagonal Court-yard, designed by Bramante. Turning to the right, between the two dogs, we come soon to the Laocoön room, in which is the famous group of Laocoön, depicting the priest of Apollo and his sons being attacked by serpents. This statue, a genuine Greek work of the first century B.C., is the subject of Lessing's great book on the æsthetics of art, which might well be read by intending visitors to Rome who care for sculpture. Julius II acquired the group on its discovery in a Roman garden, and Michael Angelo, who was one of the first persons to see it, pronounced it marvellous. When I was first in Rome, in 1895, it was covered by pencilled autographs. But either trippers' manners have improved or the custodians are more vigilant, for there are none to-day.

On the wall of the passage to the next room is a relief from the Ara Pacis, or altar of Peace, which the Senate built for the Emperor Augustus in 13 B.C., the peace being that following his campaigns against the Spanish

and the French. The position of the Altar was just off
the Corso Umberto I, near the site of the present Houses
of Parliament. In the Uffizi in Florence is the greatest
assemblage of portions of this memorial; others are in
the Terme of Diocletian. The fragmentary figure in the
central niche, of a draped woman, recalling the Winged
Victory in the Louvre, is supposed to be Greek and to
represent the daughter of Niobe escaping from the anger
of Apollo.

The next room has the Belvedere Apollo, which also
was acquired by Julius II: a triumphantly beautiful
statue. The hands are new. This is a copy of a bronze
Greek original. In the next room we find Canova attempt-
ing to be a Greek sculptor of the same period. Just
before we enter the Hermes room, note the wall relief
from a sarcophagus with the open door of the nether
world.

The beautiful Hermes was discovered in a garden in
1543 and acquired by Paul III. Nicholas Poussin called
it the most perfect example of the human male body.
The marble is of peculiar brilliance. The bas-reliefs in the
walls of this room are full of life. In this room the
Apoxyomenos of Lysippus has now been placed, a Greek
copy of a bronze which used to be in the Portico of
Agrippa, near the Pantheon. This statue was found as
recently as 1849.

We now cross to the Round Vestibule and look out of
the window for a view of Rome and the mountains. The
plain sarcophagus of Cornelius Scipio Barbatus came
from his family tomb beside the Appian Way.

The massive and powerful torso in the third and last
of these little rooms is authentic Greek work of the first
century B.C. Clement VII brought it to the Vatican.

We now pass through the Chiaramonti Museum to that
perfect gallery the Braccio Nuovo. The variety of ob-

CHAPTER IX

Raphael in Rome

Raphael's early Days—Julius II—Agostino Chigi, the Banker—
Leo X—Raphael's House—His Death—And Epitaph—The Decora-
tion of the Stanze—The Disputa—The School of Athens—The
Parnassus—The Expulsion of Heliodorus—Raphael's "Bible"—
The Picture Gallery of the Vatican—Napoleon's Conveyances—The
early Sienese Painters—A Leonardo Attribution—The Raphael
Room—Raphael's Pupils—S. Maria della Pace and Raphael's Sibyls
—Bramante's Cloister.

BEFORE we examine the frescoes painted by Raphael
for Julius II and Leo X it might be well to say something of the Roman career of this youthful genius, who
was cut down at an age when other men have hardly
come to their full strength.

Raphael's life falls very simply into three periods, the
first being from his birth in 1483 to his twenty-first year,
during which time he was growing up about the Court of
the Duke of Montefeltro (whose palace was at Urbino and
who greatly esteemed Raphael's father, Giovanni Sanzio,
both as a man and a painter) and later as apprentice to
Pietro Vannucci, called Perugino, after his home, Perugia.
The second period was from 1504 to 1508 when the youth
was in Florence, studying the frescoes of Masaccio and
Masolino, painted long since, and the contemporary cartoons which Michael Angelo and Leonardo were making
in rivalry for the Palazzo Vecchio; and receiving great
kindness and encouragement from many of the leaders
of culture and art in that city, notably Fra Bartolommeo
the painter, and Baccio d'Agnolo the architect. Before
he finally left Florence, at the age of only twenty-five, he

87

had completed such masterpieces as the "Madonna del
Granduca" now in the Pitti, the "Madonna del Cardellino"
now in the Uffizi, the "Ansidei Madonna" now in the
London National Gallery, and "La Bella Giardiniera"
now in the Louvre. In 1508, when the third and last
period begins, came an invitation to Rome from Bramante, the architect, a fellow Umbrian who was then at
work on St. Peter's for Julius II.

Already in Rome working for the Pope was Raphael's
master, Perugino, and among the other artists that Julius
had assembled were Luca Signorelli, Pinturicchio, Lorenzo
Lotto and Michael Angelo himself, all doing work for the
Pope and for his friends, among whom was Agostino
Chigi, the banker, for whom as we have seen, Raphael
was to design a chapel at S. Maria del Popolo, the family
church also of the Della Rovere family to which Julius II
belonged.

Raphael's sweetness and simplicity of character brought
him only affection; in spite of his competitive valour,
there seems to have been entertained for this brilliant
youthful stranger, with the faultless hand, no resent-
ment, no rancour. He was welcomed, and remained popular even though Julius II sacrificed old frescoes by
Piero della Francesca, Luca Signorelli, Andrea del Cas-
tagno, and others, in order to provide space for the new
recruit. Raphael viewed their destruction with repulsion;
but Popes must be obeyed. He was able, however, to save
the Peruginos, as we shall see on the ceiling of the Stanza
dell' Incendio.

Pope Julius II, under whose caprice and dominance
Michael Angelo, a less flexible character than Raphael,
suffered so deeply, died in 1503, and then came Giovanni
de' Medici to be Pope, as Leo X, whose patronage of
Raphael was as warm as his predecessor's; who consented
to Raphael being appointed Bramante's first lieutenant

THE APOLLO DEL BELVEDERE
After the Statue in the Vatican

[*See page* 82

Photograph by Anderson

SILENUS AND THE YOUTHFUL BACCHUS
*After the Statue in the Sala dei Candelabri in
the Vatican*

[*See page 83*

Photograph by Anderson

THE FAUN
    After the Statue by PRAXITELES *in the*
    Capitoline Museum

[*See page* 83

Photograph by Anderson

THE DISCOBOLUS OF MYRON
After the Statue in the Sala della Biga in
the Vatican

[See page 84

as architect of St. Peter's; and who commissioned him to decorate the Loggia with those scriptural scenes which are known as "Raphael's Bible." Meanwhile Raphael had also decorated Agostino Chigi's new villa on the banks of the Tiber, now known as the Villa Farnesina. Chigi did not require the Bible; he preferred Lemprière; and Raphael's frescoes (as we shall see) are the gayest and most brilliant scenes in the stories of the loves of the gods.

Raphael also found time to paint portraits—the Julius II is one of the best known—and various "Madonnas," large and small, such as the "Madonna of Foligno," which we shall find in the Vatican Picture Gallery, the little "Garvagh Madonna" in the London National Gallery, and the famous "Transfiguration," also at the Vatican, which he began in 1517, for the cathedral of Narbonne, but did not live to complete. At the same time Sebastiano del Piombo was painting, for the same church, the immense picture of the "Raising of Lazarus" which is now No. 1 in the London National Gallery.

Raphael's life in Rome was a series of splendours and triumphs, but he did not allow them to go to his head. His house, now destroyed, was the Palazzo di Bramante, near St. Peter's, and his two favourite pupils Giulio Romano and Gianfrancesco Penni (who completed his "Transfiguration") shared it with him. Another of his unfinished works was completed by his master Perugino, who lived on till 1523.

Raphael had been betrothed to Maria Bibbiena, the niece of Cardinal Bibbiena, but she died before him and her epitaph will be found on his own monument. Romantic rumour has made him the lover of his baker's daughter, "La Fornarina," but there are no facts.

Raphael died on Good Friday 1520, aged thirty-seven, and lay in state in the studio, with the "Transfiguration" beside his bier, while all Rome paid homage. The upkeep of his tomb was provided for in his will, from the rent of a house which you may see at No. 124 Via de' Coronari. The couplet on the tomb was composed by Cardinal Bembo, a friend of the artist. In English it might run thus:

> Nature, who feared the unequal strife
> With Raphael in his glorious life
> Was smitten with a deeper dread
> That she might die when he was dead.[1]

The frescoes in the Stanze are not easy to see even when you can adapt your position so that the light comes from behind you; but those on the walls through which the principal light comes—on the left, as you pass through—are almost invisible. And this circumstance is the more to be deplored, because they are in the best preservation, and I fancy not the least remarkable. It is impossible indeed to imagine any depiction of a miracle more vivid and persuasive than that in which the angel delivers St. Peter from prison.

In the first room we see, distinctly, on the wall opposite the window, the scene of the fire in the Borgo, as the district about St. Peter's is called. The time was the reign of Leo IV (847-855) the builder of the Leonine Wall, who is seen in the balcony at the back making the gesture which extinguished the flames. The group at the left represents—as a symbol rather than a fact—the pious Æneas carrying Anchises on his back and leading his son Ascanius from the sack of Troy. There was a good Roman reason for introducing these historic figures, as we shall see in the chapter on the Capitoline. Raphael's draughtsmanship was never stronger than here, except

[1] By Mr. C. L. Graves.

for the nude out-of-scale figure on the left. The painting was almost wholly the work of his favourite pupil, Francesco Penni. The ceiling is by Perugino.

The other wall frescoes, drawn by Raphael, but executed by his pupils, represent scenes in the reigns of Leo III and Leo IV, such as the victory of Leo IV over the Saracens; but as the commission was given to Raphael by Leo X, it is Leo X who is represented as the conqueror. With him is Cardinal Bibbiena, to whose niece Raphael became affianced. In the fresco of the Coronation of Charlemagne we find Leo X again, but this time in the place of Leo III. Flattery takes strange turnings! Note the pretty little figure kneeling on the steps. As a composition this drawing is a masterpiece.

The next room, the Stanza della Segnatura, has the masterpieces, wholly from Raphael's hand. To the right is the lovely scene called the "Disputa," which means, however, nothing acrimonious, but merely an amicable theological discussion. You discern nothing but accord among the Saints and Fathers grouped so sweetly about the altar with the hosts of heaven floating only just above their fortunate heads. This suave company of holy men against the placid tender landscape haunts the memory long after the Vatican and all its treasures are far behind.

Opposite is the "School of Athens," where the Master's ease and grace are again at their most winsome. The picture has extraordinary charm: indeed the word perfection may perhaps be used without fear. Probably every figure was meant by Raphael to represent either an ancient philosopher or a modern friend of the artist or of the Pope—in this case Julius II, for this fresco was earlier than the Leo X series; but only a few can be identified with confidence. There seems to be no doubt that the old man on the steps who cares for nobody is Diogenes. On the far right is Raphael himself with either Sodoma or Perugino. The tall youth on the left in blue with the regular, rather girlish, features, would seem to be the same as the first standing figure on the left in the "Disputa" opposite. The architectural background gives hardly less pleasure than the figures and the arrangement.

I am tempted in this room to repeat what I once said elsewhere, that no one who has seen Raphael only as a painter of altar-pieces and Madonnas has any true idea of his genius, or any right to utter opinions as to his powers. Had he remained with Perugino, the world might still have some exquisite works, but they would be marked by a certain insipidity. It was Rome that made a man of him; Rome and Julius II.

Perhaps it is in the "Parnassus," also in this room, that Raphael's ingenuity in filling odd spaces is most noticeable, for he had to contend with a lunette with a rectangular gap in it. By an inspiration he made this gap serve as a kind of pedestal for the additional glorification of Apollo, the central figure. The old man lifting his sightless eyes, on the left, is Homer; and at his right side, laurel-crowned, is Dante; on the other side, Virgil. The symbolic figures on the ceiling, also wholly Raphael's, are Theology, Philosophy, Poetry and Justice.

To my mind the masterpiece of the next room, the Stanza d'Eliodoro, is the St. Peter to which I have already referred; but you can see it only with difficulty if not pain. The Expulsion of Heliodorus from the Temple again shows us Raphael's triumphant power of hand and sense of composition. The vista of arches culminating in the landscape is like balm to the eyes, and there seems to be nothing incongruous between the arrested movement of the flying figure in the foreground and the quiet old man—the High Priest—praying at the back. At the left is Pope Julius, Raphael's patron. Of the last room, devoted to events in the life of Constantine the Great, and painted by Raphael's pupils, I speak in another chapter.

We now come to the decorated Loggia known as Raphael's Bible, where a number of scenes from the Old Testament and two or three from the New are gaily depicted, amid Pompeian patterns. Raphael here was chiefly draughtsman, his pupils, and particularly Giulio Romano, being the colourists. But there is nothing here to compare with the "Disputa" and "School of Athens." Of the joint labours of the same master and pupils at the Farnesina I shall say something in a later chapter, when we cross the Tiber.

Since Raphael is the peculiar glory of the Vatican Picture Gallery, let me speak here of that admirable collection, the present housing and arrangement of which were due to Pius X, although to Pius VI belongs the credit of forming it. Pius VII, the Pope whose misfortune it was to be on the papal throne during the Napoleonic era, had the pain of seeing the hundred best pictures of his church removed to enrich the Louvre. He had, however, the satisfaction of welcoming them back after Waterloo —but not all. One hundred were taken; only seventy-seven were disgorged.

The first room gives us church painting in its infancy, one step beyond the Byzantine altar-pieces. It is simple and often crude, but marked by gaiety and a sense of illustration. These early Sienese and Florentines were indeed far better illustrators than their more self-conscious and mature successors; and the result is that this room and, in part, the next, are really a pictorial version, often very vivid, of the Lives of the Saints. The work of Sano di Pietro should be looked for, also Nos. 17 and 18 "in the manner of Lorenzo di Nicolò," an Annunciation and a Nativity; and for freshness, gaiety and

93

unaffected charm, Nos. 127 and 128, the "Banquet of Herod" and "Salome receiving the Head of John the Baptist."

And of course you will look for the Fra Angelicos. But the place, in Rome, for this painter is the chapel of Nicholas V, adjoining Raphael's Stanze, where his hand is stronger than in any of these pictorial beatitudes. It was while working on them that he died, and that is why Rome has his body in its keeping—in the church of the Minerva, just across the road from Raphael's tomb in the Pantheon.

The Annunciation panel of the predella, beneath the Gozzoli altar-piece No. 123, is also delightful: the news being broken in a Florentine garden. It is in this room that the Melozzo da Forli studies and his portrait of Sixtus IV are to be found; but his sophistication seems to jar after the happy impulses of the primitives.

A greater contrast is obtained by comparing the careful colouring of Cossa's scenes in the life of St. Vincent with any of those earlier recorders. Illustration has gone out: art has come in.

The unfinished picture of St. Jerome with his lion, so different from the meek, unleonine, and often cross-bred animal that too often accompanies this Saint, may be by Leonardo da Vinci, as the catalogue suggests. I see no reason why it should not be.

The Venetian room has a very interesting putative Giovanni Bellini, a Pietà, as strong as his brother-in-law Mantegna, but softer too; and, next it, a Crivelli, a painter who leaves you in no possible doubt as to the authorship of his works. And there is a mellow Doge with Titian's name. In the last room the English visitors come, with a kind of shock, on a big courtier-like portrait of George IV by Sir Thomas Lawrence, who was a personage in Rome towards the end of his brilliant career.

94

RAPHAEL IN ROME

And now for Raphael's room, in which are his "Transfiguration," his last work, finished by his pupils, his "Madonna da Foligno," his "Crowning of the Virgin," and some lighter works. To my eyes the most pleasing is the "Madonna da Foligno," which was painted for Sigismundo, Conte da Foligno, to celebrate his escape from a bomb, and at first was placed over the altar at the Santa Maria in Aracœli. Then it went to a church in Foligno, and then was conveyed by Napoleon to the Louvre. All Raphael's perfect drawing, skill in composition and seraphic sweetness are here.

The "Transfiguration" is, of course, far more remarkable, for there the artist had to depict the most dramatic moment in all history and fix that moment without sacrifice of repose. He has certainly triumphed. Why should Christ be ascending and not descending? But ascending undoubtedly He is; and not because we know the story, but because the artist makes it so. There is plenty of action in the frescoes which we have been looking at in the Stanze; but in his easel pictures Raphael prefers quiescence and placidity to action. Here, however, he seems to have had thoughts of trying conclusions with Michael Angelo. The kneeling woman in the foreground could not have been done better by that Master.

This is the picture which Raphael desired to be placed beside his death bed. It was commissioned by Cardinal Giulio de' Medici, afterwards Clement VII, and given by him to S. Pietro in Montorio, where it was the chief altarpiece until Napoleon thought it would look better in the Louvre.

Raphael's pupils, Giulio Romano and Francesco Penni, completed the "Transfiguration." You see how they painted, when independent, in their version of the Madonna's vacated tomb; so much more commonplace than Raphael's with its single lily. You see here also the

A WANDERER IN ROME

likeness of Raphael's master, Perugino, to his pupil, until
his pupil found his wings.

On our way back we might pause at the Pantheon to
pay homage to Raphael's tomb. If we stop on the way
at the church of S. Maria della Pace we shall find one other
sacred fresco by the Master—the Sibyls. S. Maria della
Pace is one of the most comely of the smaller churches
of Rome, calm and imposing, with a fine lofty dome and
a massive colonnade; but it is hemmed in by very dirty
houses. It was built by Sixtus IV in 1484 and completed
by Alexander VII (the Chigi Pope), the peacefulness of
whose reign (1665-1667) its name commemorates. The
first chapel on the right was the gift of the same Agostino Chigi for whom Raphael painted the mythological
series and for whom he designed the Chigi chapel at S.
Maria del Popolo. Behind the faded curtains which the
sacristan pulls aside is the fresco of the Sibyls, one of
the Master's suavest works. You will note again his
genius for filling odd spaces and his affection for rich
yellows. As a contrast to Raphael's bland sweetness,
ask the sacristan to show you the cloisters of the young
painter's friend and patron Bramante, so severe and
cool.

MUSIC
After the fresco by PINTURICCHIO *in the Borgia Apartments in the Vatican*

[*See page* 86

THE CREATION

After the painting by RAPHAEL *in the Loggia of the Vatican*

[*See page* 89

CHAPTER X

Michael Angelo in Rome

The Omnipresent Hand—A Masterful Pope—Vasari's *Lives*—
Preparations for a Papal Tomb—The horned Moses—The Ceiling
of the Sistine Chapel—Artist *versus* Pope—A wheeled Couch—
Vasari's Criticism—The Last Judgment—The Portrait of Michael
Angelo—Shakespeare's Birth.

SO much of the Rome that we admire was the work of
Michael Angelo—the Sistine Chapel paintings not
the least, although perhaps the least permanent—that
this is a fitting place to tell his story.

His greatest contribution to the Eternal City was the
dome of St. Peter's, but to him it owes also the Pietà in
that church, the Christ in S. Maria sopra Minerva, the
tomb of Julius II with the figure of Moses, portions of
the Farnese palace, the Piazza of the Campidoglio,
the church and cloisters of S. Maria degli Angeli transformed from the Baths of Diocletian, and the Porta Pia.
The Master was also behind the scenes in many another
architectural work, while among the many minor activities attributed to Michael Angelo is the design of the
Swiss Guard's uniform. But on this matter of Michael
Angelo's variety and ubiquity the last words were said by
the author of *The Innocents Abroad*.

When Michael Angelo came to Rome from Florence,
in 1505, at the bidding of Pope Julius II, who had heard
of the genius of the artist and desired a marvellous tomb
from his hand to be set in the place of honour in the new
church of St. Peter which he was projecting, he was

thirty. At the moment of the papal summons he was busy with the cartoons for the Palazzo Vecchio, of which I have just spoken; but Popes must be obeyed, and particularly this ambitious, energetic and changeable-minded one, to whose autocratic whims Michael Angelo, as it turned out, was to sacrifice so much peace of mind and possibly so many masterpieces.

The story of the conflict of wills between the Pope and the man of genius is one of the most interesting in the history of art, and we have good authority for it in Giorgio Vasari's pages. That writer, the biographer of the great Italian painters and himself a fair practitioner with the brush, may too often give credence to information gained at second-hand and from untrustworthy sources, but the statements in his memoir of Michael Angelo, or Michelagnolo, can be relied upon, because he was a confidant and disciple of the Master, and worked in his studio. I quote, by permission, here as elsewhere in the book, from a new translation of the *Lives*, by Gaston Du C. de Vere.[1]

Vasari tells us that Michael Angelo began his work for Julius by visiting the quarries of Carrara. "There, in those mountains, he spent eight months without other moneys or supplies; and he had many fantastic ideas of carving great statues in those quarries, in order to leave memorials of himself, as the ancients had done before him, being invited by those masses of stone. Then, having picked out the due quantity of marbles, he caused them to be loaded on board ship at the coast and then conveyed to Rome, where they filled half the Piazza di S. Pietro, round about S. Caterina, and between the church and the corridor that goes to the Castello. In that place Michelagnolo had prepared his room for executing the

[1] *Lives of the Most Eminent Painters*, by Giorgio Vasari. In 10 volumes. The Medici Society.

gone to see it several times (mounting certain ladders with the assistance of Michelagnolo) insisted that it should be thrown open, for he was hasty and impatient by nature, and could not wait for it to be completely finished and to receive, as the saying is, the final touch. No sooner was it thrown open than all Rome was drawn to see it, and the Pope was the first, not having the patience to wait until the dust caused by the dismantling of the scaffolding had settled. Thereupon Raffaello da Urbino, who was very excellent in imitation, after seeing it straightway changed his manner, and without losing any time, in order to display his ability, painted the Prophets and Sibyls in the work of the Pace; and at the same time Bramante sought to have the other half of the chapel entrusted by the Pope to Raffaello. Which hearing, Michelagnolo complained of Bramante, and revealed to the Pope without any reserve many faults both in his life and his architectural works; of which last, in the building of S. Pietro, as was seen afterwards, Michelagnolo became the corrector.

"But the Pope, recognizing more clearly every day the ability of Michelagnolo, desired that he should continue the work, judging, after he had seen it uncovered, that he could make the second half considerably better; and so in twenty months he carried that work to perfect completion by himself alone, without the assistance even of any one to grind his colours. Michelagnolo complained at times that on account of the haste that the Pope imposed on him he was not able to finish it in his own fashion, as he would have liked; for His Holiness was always asking him importunately when he would finish it. On one occasion, among others, he replied. 'It will be finished when I shall have satisfied myself in the matter of art.' 'But it is our pleasure,' answered the Pope, 'that you should satisfy us in our desire to have it done quickly';

and he added, finally, that if Michelagnolo did not finish
the work quickly he would have him thrown from the
scaffolding. Whereupon Michelagnolo, who feared, and
had good reason to fear, the anger of the Pope, straightway finished all that was wanting, without losing any
time, and, after taking down the rest of the scaffolding,
threw it open to view on the morning of All Saints' Day,
when the Pope went into the chapel to sing Mass, to the
great satisfaction of the whole city.

"Michelagnolo desired to retouch some parts 'a secco,'
as the old masters had done on the scenes below, painting
backgrounds, draperies, and skies in ultramarine, and
ornaments in gold in certain places, to the end that this
might produce greater richness and a more striking effect; and the Pope, having learned that this ornamentation was wanting, and hearing the work praised so much
by all who had seen it, wished him to finish it; but, since
it would have been too long a labour for Michelagnolo to
rebuild the scaffolding, it was left as it was. His Holiness,
often seeing Michelagnolo, would say to him that the
chapel should be enriched with colours and gold, since
it looked poor. And Michelagnolo would answer famil-
iarly, 'Holy Father, in those times men did not bedeck
themselves with gold, and those that are painted there
were never very rich, but rather holy men, on which account they despised riches.'

"For this work Michelagnolo was paid by the Pope
three thousand crowns on several occasions, of which he
had to spend twenty-five on colours. The work was executed with very great discomfort to himself, from his
having to labour with his face upwards, which so im-
paired his sight that for a time, which was not less than
several months, he was not able to read letters or look
at drawings save with his head backwards. And to this I
can bear witness, having painted five vaulted chambers

THE SCHOOL OF ATHENS
After the Picture by RAPHAEL *in the Stanze of the Vatican*

[*See page* 91

Photograph by Anderson

THE LIBERATION OF ST. PETER
After the fresco by RAPHAEL *in the*
Stanze of the Vatican

[*See page* 92

Photograph by Hanfstaengl

THE MADONNA DI FOLIGNO
After the picture by RAPHAEL *in the
Picture Gallery of the Vatican*

[*See page* 95

THE TRANSFIGURATION
After the picture by RAPHAEL *in the
Picture Gallery of the Vatican*

[*See page* 95

in the great apartments in the Palace of Duke Cosimo, when, if I had not made a chair on which I could rest my head and lie down at my work, I would never have finished it; even so, it has so ruined my sight and injured my head, that I still feel the effects, and I am astonished that Michelagnolo endured all that discomfort so well. But in truth, becoming more and more kindled every day by his fervour in the work, and encouraged by the proficience and improvement that he made, he felt no fatigue and cared nothing for discomfort."

The paintings are not easy to see, unless one defies public opinion and, following the painter's example, lies, face-upwards, on the floor. As I have written elsewhere, although the mirror which the attendant supplies is a help, only a couch on wheels, like a stretcher-chair, on which one might lie on one's back and be slowly moved and turned hither and thither, would really solve the problem. Perhaps the Pope has such an article for personal use? If I lived in Rome I should crave permission to bring one to the chapel with me. Thus placed, and thus only, one could rightly study the superhuman wonders of this feat of decoration and realize how in every department of painting, Michael Angelo could, had he been less of a colossus and less disdainful, have succeeded. The scene in which Adam is tempted is, for example, such a piece of tender romantic landscape as we associate with the name of Giorgione.

Each visitor to the Sistine Chapel—and visiting it should become a habit—will find his own way among the designs, but the good Vasari is so enthusiastic that I should like to quote him a little more: "This work, in truth, has been and still is, the lamp of our art, and has bestowed such benefits and shed so much light on the art of painting, that it has served to illuminate a world that had lain in darkness for so many hundreds of years. And

it is certain that no man who is a painter need think any
more to see new inventions, attitudes and draperies for
the clothing of figures, novel manners of expression, and
things painted with greater variety and force, because he
gave to this work all the perfection that can be given
to any work executed in such a field of art. And at the
present day every one is amazed who is able to perceive
in it the excellence of the figures, the perfection of the
foreshortenings, and the extraordinary roundness of the
contours, which have in them slenderness and grace, being drawn with the beauty of proportion that is seen in
beautiful nudes; and these, in order to display the supreme perfection of art, he made of all ages, different in
expression and in form, in countenance and in outline,
some more slender and some fuller in the members; as
may also be seen in the beautiful attitudes, which are all
different, some seated, some moving, and others upholding
certain festoons of oak-leaves and acorns, placed there
as the arms and device of Pope Julius, and signifying
that at that time and under his government was the age
of gold; for Italy was not then in the travail and misery
that she has since suffered. Between them, also, they
hold some medallions containing stories in relief in imitation of bronze and gold, taken from the Book of Kings.

"Besides this, in order to display the perfection of art
and also the greatness of God, he painted in a scene God
dividing Light from Darkness, wherein may be seen His
Majesty as He rests self-sustained with the arms outstretched, and reveals both love and power. In the second
scene he depicted with the most beautiful judgment and
genius God creating the Sun and Moon, in which He is supported by many little Angels, in an attitude sublime and
terrible by reason of the foreshortenings in the arms and
legs. In the same scene Michelagnolo depicted Him after
the Blessing of the Earth and the Creation of the Animals,

MICHAEL ANGELO IN ROME

when He is seen on that vaulting as a figure flying in
foreshortening; and wherever you go throughout the
chapel, it turns constantly and faces in every direction.
So, also, in the next scene, where He is dividing the Water
from the Earth; and both these are very beautiful figures
and refinements of genius such as could be produced only
by the divine hands of Michelagnolo.

"He then went on, beyond that scene, to the Creation
of Adam, wherein he figured God as borne by a group of
nude Angels of tender age, which appear to be supporting
not one figure only, but the whole weight of the world;
this effect being produced by the venerable majesty of
His form and by the manner of the movement with which
He embraces some of the little Angels with one arm, as if
to support Himself, and with the other extends the right
hand towards Adam, a figure of such a kind in its beauty,
in the attitude, and in the outlines, that it appears as if
newly fashioned by the first and supreme Creator rather
than by the brush and design of a mortal man. Beyond
this, in another scene, he made God taking our mother
Eve from Adam's side, in which may be seen those two
nude figures, one as it were dead from his being the thrall
of sleep, and the other become alive and filled with anima-
tion by the blessing of God. Very clearly do we see from
the brush of this most gifted craftsman the difference that
there is between sleep and wakefulness, and how firm and
stable, speaking humanly, the Divine Majesty may
appear."

Of the Isaiah, Vasari says: "The Prophet Isaiah, wholly
absorbed in his own thoughts, has the legs crossed over
one another, and, holding one hand in his book to mark
the place where he was reading, has placed the elbow of
the other arm upon the book, with the cheek pressed
against the hand; and, being called by one of the boys
that he has behind him, he turns only the head, without

disturbing himself otherwise. Whoever shall consider his countenance, shall see touches truly taken from Nature herself, the true mother of art, and a figure which, when well studied in every part, can teach in liberal measure all the precepts of the good painter. Beyond this Prophet is an aged Sibyl of great beauty, who, as she sits, studies from a book in an attitude of extraordinary grace, not to speak of the beautiful attitudes of the two boys that are about her. Nor may any man think with all his imaginings to be able to attain to the excellence of the figure of a youth representing Daniel, who, writing in a great book, is taking certain things from other writings and copying them with extraordinary attention; and as a support for the weight of the book Michelagnolo painted a boy between his legs, who is upholding it while he writes, all which no brush held by a human hand, however skilful, will ever be able to equal. And so, also, with the beautiful figure of the Libyan Sibyl, who, having written a great volume drawn from many books, is in an attitude of womanly grace, as if about to rise to her feet; and in one and the same movement she makes as if to rise and to close the book—a thing most difficult, not to say impossible, for any other but the master of the work."

So much for the ceiling. The other work by Michael Angelo, "The Last Judgment" on the end wall, belongs to a much later date. After the completion of the Sistine ceiling in 1511 or 1512 Michael Angelo was again busy with Julius's tomb, now less magnificent in scheme, and was sufficiently harassed; but when in 1513 Julius died his worries were increased, because the Pope's heirs wished to diminish the tomb still more and spend far less money, and the artist was already heavily out of pocket.

The death of Julius in 1513 was by no means the end of Papal influences in Michael Angelo's magnificent if melancholy and frustrated career. Julius's successor, Leo

MICHAEL ANGELO IN ROME

X, one of the Medici, whom he had known as a boy, sent him to Florence, and one of Leo's successors, another member of the Medici family, Clement VII, kept him there. We may be glad that they did so, for the beautiful and sublime Medici chapel was the result; but the tomb of Julius was to suffer.

It was not until 1534 that Michael Angelo was again in Rome, when a further effort upon the Julius tomb, still more reduced in scope, would have been begun, had not the new Pope, Paul III, insisted on "The Last Judgment" being added to the Sistine Chapel, although not forgetting that the Farnese palace, then being built, should receive attention too. For seven years the artist worked at it, and in 1541 it was unveiled. Says Vasari: "Wherefore he who has judgment and understanding in painting perceives there the most terrible force of art, and sees in those figures such thoughts and passions as were never painted by any other but Michelagnolo. So, also, he may see there how the variety of innumerable attitudes is accomplished, in the strange and diverse gestures of young and old, male and female; and who is there who does not recognize in these the terrible power of his art, together with the grace that he had from Nature, since they move the hearts not only of those who have knowledge in that profession, but even of those who have none? There are foreshortenings that appear as if in relief, a harmony of painting that gives great softness, and fineness in the parts painted by him with delicacy, all showing in truth how pictures executed by good and true painters should be; and in the outlines of the forms turned by him in such a way as could not have been achieved by another but Michelagnolo, may be seen the true Judgment and the true Damnation and Resurrection. This is for our art the exemplar and the grand manner of painting sent down to men on earth by God, to the end that they may see how Destiny works when intellects descend from the heights of Heaven to earth, and have infused in them divine grace and knowledge.

"This work leads after it bound in chains those who persuade themselves that they have mastered art; and at the sight of the strokes drawn by him in the outlines of no matter what figure, every sublime spirit, however mighty in design, trembles and is afraid. And while the eyes gaze at his labours in this work, the senses are numbed at the mere thought of what manner of things all other pictures, those painted and those still unpainted, would appear if placed in comparison with such perfection. Truly blessed may he be called, and blessed his memories, who has seen this truly stupendous marvel of our age! Most happy and most fortunate Paul III, in that God granted that under thy protection should be acquired the renown that the pens of writers shall give to his memory and thine! How highly are thy merits enhanced by his genius! And what good fortune have the craftsmen had in this age from his birth, in that they have seen the veil of every difficulty torn away, and have beheld in the pictures, sculptures, and architectural works executed by him all that can be imagined and achieved!"

Although the artist was old and tired, the Pope did not allow him to remain idle, and first set him upon designing the fortifications of the Borgo and then completing St. Peter's, which had become a happy hunting ground for venal contractors; and that glory of the world, its dome, was the result.

And what was the creator of these marvels like? Here is Vasari's description of him in later life: "He was of middle stature, broad in the shoulders, but well proportioned in all the rest of his body. In his latter years he wore buskins of doeskin on the legs, next to the skin, constantly for whole months together, so that afterwards, when he sought to take them off, on drawing them off the skin often came away with them. Over the stockings he wore boots of cordwain fastened on the inside as a protection against damp. His face was round, the brow square and spacious, with seven straight lines, and the temples projected considerably beyond the ears; which ears were somewhat on the large side, and stood out from the cheeks. The body was in proportion to the face, or rather on the large side; the nose somewhat flattened, as was said in the Life of Torrigiano, who broke it for him with his fist; his eyes rather on the small side, of the colour of horn, spotted with blueish and yellowish gleams; the eyebrows with few hairs, the lips thin, with the lower lip rather thicker and projecting a little, the chin well shaped and in proportion with the rest, the hair black, but mingled with white hairs, like the beard, which was not very long, forked, and not very thick.

"Truly," Vasari adds, "his coming was to the world, as I said at the beginning, an exemplar sent by God to the men of our arts, to the end that they might learn from his life the nature of noble character, and from his works what true and excellent craftsmen ought to be."

Michael Angelo died in 1564, the year in which Shakespeare was born.

CHAPTER XI

Small Picture Galleries and a Great Church

IF we bear to the right, at the top step of the Scala
di Spagna, we come at once to the beginning of the
Via Sistina, which runs direct down hill, up hill and
so forth, undulatingly, to the great church of S. Maria
Maggiore, changing its name, in the Roman manner, two
or three times on the way. The first change of name is
at the Piazza Barberini on the Quirinal hill, where the
fountain of the Triton stands, one of Bernini's masterpieces, and here the street becomes the Via delle Quattro
Fontane.

A little way along on the left we come to the entrance
of the Palazzo Barberini, another work of Bernini's, built
for the same Pope, Urban VIII, who gave St. Peter's its
baldacchino. Here is a picture gallery, with a few notable works in it. But very few. Rome's best pictures
are the frescoes on its walls. The gallery has a vogue
on account of Guido Reni's famous head of Beatrice
Cenci and the "Fornarina" of Raphael. Both descrip-
tions are, however, doubtful. The Fornarina may be any
one but the baker's daughter of romance, and the Beatrice
Cenci is probably one of the sibyls. At any rate there
are sibyls by the same painter who might easily belong

THE CREATION OF MAN
After the fresco by MICHAEL ANGELO *in the*
Sistine Chapel

[*See page* 106

DANIEL

Photograph by Brogi

THE PROPHET DANIEL
After the fresco by MICHAEL ANGELO
in the Sistine Chapel

[*See page* 108

to the same series, wearing the head-dress assigned to them by tradition. We have one in the Wallace Collection. On the other hand, the picture postcard shops in Rome sell a popular reproduction of a modern work by an artist named Leonardi, of Guido Reni actually in the act of making this portrait, visiting Beatrice in her prison cell for the purpose, while warders look on. Beatrice is at her crucifix, and her head unmistakably wears the turban of the paintings. So what shall we say?

A good Andrea del Sarto and Dürer's curious representation of the Boy Christ among the scribes remain in the memory. Two pieces of statuary are noteworthy: the "Suppliant," a genuine Greek work of the fifth century B.C. in Room I, and in the garden a statue by Thorwaldsen, the Danish sculptor (1770-1844), who worked for many years in Rome, and whose house was close by at No. 48 Via Sistina.

At the Four Fountains themselves (which are not bravely set in the midst of an open space, but fixed to the walls) the street comes to the point where the Via Venti Settembre branches off to the left and the Via del Quirinale to the right. The Via Venti Settembre, which we will not now take, named in honour of the day on which Rome was joined to the Kingdom of Italy, in 1870, is the Whitehall of Rome, for it contains the great Government departments.

The Via del Quarinale leads to the Royal Palace, and if we were to turn down this street we should come, on the left, to the church of S. Andrea from designs by Bernini. The adjoining house of the Noviceship is now government property, but the sanctity of S. Stanislaus Kostka is still cherished there, while in the church is his shrine. The church should be peeped into for its beautiful columns of red marble and white Sicilian jasper. Next it is a public garden with a statue of the father of Vittorio

A WANDERER IN ROME

Emmanuele II in its midst, while opposite is the Royal
Palace, with its green garden stretching behind, glimpses
of which you get through an open doorway. It is under
this pleasaunce that the Tunnel runs, through which
every Roman cabman too often takes you. This tunnel
nominally was made as a short cut between the Via Tritone
and the Via Nazionale, but actually (I suspect)
because the Romans did not find any of their existing
thoroughfares noisy enough.

The palace of the Quirinale began its existence as a
papal residence in the sixteenth century under Gregory
XIII and so continued until 1870. Its proudest tenant
was Paul V (1605-1621) the Borghese, who made it magnificent and added its Chapel of the Annunciation. Urban
VIII (1623-1644), who died here, built the Balcony of
Benediction and the new entrance, Bernini being, as usual,
his architect. Alexander VII (1655-1667) also called
in Bernini to help with extensions. Pius IX (1846-1878)
was the last Pope to live here and to pronounce public
blessings.

The glorious horse-tamers that guard the obelisk originally stood in front of Constantine's baths, which were
situated on this hill; the obelisk itself is from the mausoleum of Augustus. From the terrace in front of the piazza
of the palace, looking towards St. Peter's you have a fine
view of Rome. The huge, sombre buildings of the steep
and narrow Via della Dataria, which takes you down to
the Corso, were once papal offices, and are now barracks.
The Royal Palace and the royal stables, which are diag-
onally opposite, are shown on fixed days, but I have
never entered them. The great palace in a courtyard to
the left of the Via del Quirinale is the Rospigliosi, where
Guido Reni's "Aurora," a ceiling painting, is found.
Guido Reni's hand we see in many churches in Rome, but
this is perhaps his best work and certainly his most

pleasing. Not a painter of the first rank—or, at any rate, not an artist of the first rank—he was, in his time, one of Rome's favourite decorators. Born at Bologna in 1575, he worked in Rome for twenty years and left only through a quarrel with one of his Cardinal patrons. Ruskin found in him a "few pale rays of fading sanctity," but it is possible to miss even those. But I have seen masterly drawings from his pencil.

The garden on the other side of the Via del Quirinale, facing the Rospigliosi palace, is that of the Villa Colonna, the palazzo being reached by bridges over the Via della Pilotta. The palace itself adjoins the church of the Twelve Apostles, and since we are so near I might say a word here about the Colonna pictures, which are largely Venetian and not of the highest order, but which include a series of landscapes by Gaspard Poussin, pupil and name-child of the great Nicholas.

I have said something of the attractions of Rome to Claude Lorraine. To his contemporary, Nicholas Poussin (1593-1665), who reached the Holy City in 1624 and remained there until 1640, it was equally potent. A brief and illustrious interlude in Paris followed, when he was made court painter to Louis XIII, but in 1643 he was back in Rome once more, and, like Claude, he died here. Poussin's tomb is in the church of S. Lorenzo in Lucina, just off the Corso; his "Metamorphosis of Daphne" (Bernini's subject in sculpture at the Villa Umberto I) hangs in this gallery. Gaspard Poussin (really Gaspard Dughet, a brother of Nicholas's wife), was born in 1613 and worked in Rome and its neighbourhood all his life. At the National Gallery we have many of his fine Italian oils; the Colonna treasures are in water-colour.

And now we will resume the broken walk towards S. Maria Maggiore, to gain which, after leaving the Four

Fountains, we must cross the Via Nazionale, always keeping straight ahead.

Santa Maria Maggiore, on the Esquiline hill, is yet another óf the incredibly vast churches of Rome, placed, as so many of them are not, in an open space, so that its external proportions also can be grasped. Before we enter it, let me say that the column in the piazza is one of eight from the basilica of Constantine, that huge ruin in the Forum with the three gigantic arches.

The church of Santa Maria Maggiore, according to the legend, was set on this spot in obedience to a vision which came simultaneously to Pope Liberius and to a godly Roman named Johannes, on August 4, 342, in which the Virgin, manifesting herself to them, bade them establish a church on that spot in Rome, where, on the next day, they should find snow. Snow in Rome in midwinter is exceptional: in August it is sufficiently rare for ordinary sinful men, even thus celestially forewarned, to go to sleep secure in their minds against another builders' bill. But Pope Liberius and Johannes had virtue, and, knowing the rules, credulity, and no doubt when they awoke the next morning were not surprised to find the ground white. As it happened, on that particular night snow had fallen just here, and so the church began. A mosaic of their vision will be found on the façade, while the high altar is reputed to be Johannes's tomb.

As we now see it, the church is the result of rebuildings and extensions under various Popes, whose tombs are here; and magnificent is the only word. Gregory IX added the campanile. The chief treasure of Santa Maria Maggiore is a portion of the identical manger in which the Infant Christ lay in the stable of the inn at Bethlehem; and one Christmas Eve, at midnight, I saw this sacred relic being carried round the church in procession, by candlelight, to solemn music. Another treasure is a portrait of the Virgin by St. Luke, who was both painter and physician. This you will find over the altar of lapis lazuli in the Borghese chapel in the left transept; other pictures by St. Luke are to be seen elsewhere in Rome, placing him among those artists who are pious rather than masterly. Another treasure in the Borghese chapel is a miraculous image of the Virgin, one of the special saviours of the Roman people.

The gold on the sumptuous ceiling of the church is said to be the first brought from America. Indeed, Columbus himself is credited with having presented it. Little can it have been guessed at that time, at the end of the fifteenth century, that one day the Americans would possess in Rome a church all their own, as they have in the Via Nazionale, or that the Ludovisi quarter would become (as it now is) a suburb of New York.

Among Rome's myriad churches eighty are dedicated to the Virgin, and of these S. Maria Maggiore is, as its name suggests, the greatest. Like St. Peter's and the Lateran it has its Porta Santa; it also has its buried Popes. We come at once, at the beginning of the nave, on the left, to the tomb of Nicholas IV (1288-1292) and, on the right, to Clement IX (1667-1669).

Nicholas IV, the first Franciscan to become Pope—and one does not see St. Francis himself in that position—was of very negative character as a pontiff, whatever he may have been as a man. Clement IX, a member of the Rospigliosi family and one of the gentlest of men, had a brief reign of such clemency that the name chosen by him was fully justified.

The first chapel in the right aisle is the Baptistery, with a porphyry font and the bust of a negro,—a visitor King from the Congo, whom Urban VIII created Marquis of Nigritia,—by Bernini. In the sacristy, just here, are some reliefs by Mino da Fiesole which should be sought for.

We now come to the chapel of the Crucifix and next, in the right transept, to the Sistine Chapel, in the Confessio of which, in an attitude of prayer, is a figure of S. Gaetano by Bernini. S. Gaetano (1480-1543) was an active priest who founded the Order of Theatines and was canonized in 1671.

The praying Pope in the Confessio, before the high altar of the church, is Pius IX (1846-1878), the famous Pio Nono, whose long reign embraced so much modern history, the predecessor of Leo XIII. Of him I speak in the chapter on St. Peter's.

The tombs of two Popes are here. On the right is Pius V (1566-1572), a member of the Ghislieri family and chief of the Inquisition, who brought to his office a severity of conduct and stern simplicity of life very unusual in Popes of that time. The great event of his reign was the naval Battle of Lepanto and the conquest of the Cross over the Crescent, in 1571, the victorious commander being Marc Antonio Colonna, of the ancient Colonna house. Pius V, who was constant in his personal piety and his punishment of heretics, died from the exertion of ascending on his knees the Scala Santa at the Lateran. It was he who informed our Good Queen Bess that she was deposed from the throne; but without much disturbing that strong-minded lady.

On the other side of the chapel is the tomb of Sixtus V (1585-1590), one of the greater names in the history of the Papacy. A gardener's son, named Felice Peretti, he was self-educated until he joined the Franciscans. Becoming a preacher of eloquence, or at any rate very clear in his reasoning, he attracted the notice of Cardinal Ghislieri the Inquisitor (afterwards Pius V) who gave him the post of Vicar-General of the Franciscans. He then passed to Cardinal and Pope, his rule being notable for the sternness with which he hounded robbers and rooted out abuses, even among the Sacred Collegians. One of his failures was his support of the Spanish Armada, but he was astute enough not to pledge himself too far. He did much rebuilding and, restoring the Aqueduct of Severus, brought the Aqua Felice into Rome, to the fountain by the Grand Hotel. It was he who erected the obelisks in front of St. Peter's and beside the Lateran. It was he who had so little respect for antiquity that he set St. Peter on Trajan's column and St. Paul on that of Marcus Aurelius in the Piazza della Colonna, pulling down the two Emperors without a tremor. Indeed, most of the Rome that we see and admire to-day, began with him; and also much of the Rome that we should like to see was demolished by him.

It is in the Confessio that the remains of the Bethlehem manger are preserved. Note the Mino da Fiesole reliefs over the high altar.

The chapel in the left transept, corresponding with the Sistine in the right, is the Borghese and it is over its elaborate altar that you will see the picture by St. Luke of the Virgin, now very dark. This portrait was carried by Gregory the Great in procession through the city, and no doubt it was in his arms when, on his penitential pilgrimage to stay the plague in 590, he suddenly saw in a vision the figure of St. Michael on the top of the Castel Sant' Angelo.

The two Popes who have monuments here are, on the left, Paul V (1605-1621), one of the Borghese family, who built the chapel and, on the right, Clement VIII (1592-1605), one of the Aldobrandini, whose family palace is that enisled building in the midst of its gardens— all apparently set on a fortress—at the foot of the Via Nazionale.

A WANDERER IN ROME

Clement VIII, although the fourth Pope after Sixtus V, came to the throne only two years later; for Urban VII (1590), Gregory XIV (1590-1591) and Innocent IX (1591) had the briefest reigns. Clement VIII came to power in a period of great internal restlessness, when Italy was full of bandits and bellicose chieftains, but he did very well, and one of the triumphs of his reign was the romanizing of Henri IV, who, after a glorious career as a fighting Protestant, joined the Church of Rome in 1593 as a political move. The event is celebrated in the cloisters.

The church of St. Praxed's, where Browning's Bishop proposed to be buried, is just across the way from S. Maria Maggiore. The remains of the patron saint Praxedes and of her sister Pudentiana are preserved in a sarcophagus in the Confessio beneath the high altar, and we see them in the mosaics of the apse. In the shrine within one of the side chapels is a portion of a pillar, said to be that to which Christ was bound when He was scourged.

Praxedes and Pudentiana were the grand-daughters of a senator named Quintus Cornelius Pudens, who, if St. Peter was ever in Rome, was for some years his host; and at S. Pudenziana, in the Via Urbana, a table at which St. Peter said Mass is kept. It was Pudens's wife, afterwards known as St. Priscilla, who gave her name to the catacombs. The son of Pudens—St. Pudens—was the father of the two sisters, and his wife was Claudia Rufina from Britain. The two sisters won their saintly crowns for their efforts in preserving the bodies of the martyrs for decent burial, the well to which they conveyed the remains now being in S. Pudenziana's church. To return to her sister's fane, I may say that it is now in rather a shabby condition, with two many mediocre wall paintings. In fact, what it needs is just such a magnificent tomb as Browning's Bishop specified.

ST. PETER'S FROM THE JANICULUM HILL

[*See page* 48

SMALL PICTURE GALLERIES

From the façade of S. Maria Maggiore, to the left, a broad road, the Via Carlo Alberti, runs to the church of the Santa Croce. The gardens that interrupt this road, the Piazza Vittorio Emmanuele, contain an ancient water-tower of the Aqua Julia, called the Trofei di Mario, the trophies being the statues now at the top of the approach to the Campidoglio, beside the horse-tamers. There are some arches of the Julian Aqueduct between this spot and the railway line, just off the Viale Principessa Margherita.

From S. Maria Maggiore another broad road, more to the right, the Via Merulana, runs straight to the Lateran, whose obelisk can be seen at the far end. The great palace on the right, just past the Via Giovanni Lanza, is the Brancaccio, the gardens of which are on the site of the Baths of Trajan and Nero's Golden House, and it was here that the Laocoön group was discovered.

Just behind the Palazzo Brancaccio, in the Via Giovanni Lanza, is the church of S. Martino ai Monti, which also stands on the site of Trajan's Baths and probably incorporates some of that structure. The church (which has a series of frescoes by Gaspard Poussin—really landscapes, but purporting to tell the story of the prophet Elias) is supposed to be built on that earlier one, represented now by the crypt, in which Pope Sylvester, who baptized Constantine the Great, officiated. This church is far better worth visiting than St. Praxed's, both for its architecture (it has four and twenty noble columns) and its history. The St. Martin was no less a figure than the famous soldier who gave half his cloak to the shivering beggar and afterwards became Bishop of Tours. The St. Martin whose remains lie beneath the high altar is, as it happens, a totally different one—Pope Martin I (649-655).

121

The two strange towers that we see, one on either side of the Via Giovanni Lanza, belong to the Middle Ages, when the leading families of Rome led a life of factional rivalry and each had its stronghold.

CHAPTER XII

The Palazzo Venezia to the Tiber

A Venetian Palace—A Venetian Church—The Founder of the
Jesuits—Ecclesiastical Sumptuousness and Simplicity—The Church
of St. George of England—Carlo Maratta—The Pasquino and the
Marforio—The Piazza Navona—Bernini's Fountains—The four
Rivers—St. Agnes—A Child Martyr—Giordano Bruno—The Palazzo
Farnese—A tiny Museum—The Tiber—Modern and Ancient Rome
—S. Maria in Cosmedin—The Temple of Vesta.

THE Palazzo Venezia, the great brown building on
the Piazza Venezia, was erected by a wealthy Venetian Cardinal named Pietro Barbo, who afterwards become Pope Paul II. It was first called the Palazzio di
S. Marco, and was intended as a home for the Venetian
Cardinals, whom Barbo thought were insufficiently considered in Rome; and after serving as an ecclesiastical
palace and as the abode of the ambassador from the
Venetian Republic, the Palazzo passed to Austria. It is
now the property of the Italian Government, and may
be converted into a public art gallery.

Within the Palazzo Venezia is the ancient basilica of St.
Mark, the church of the Venetian colony. Here you find
Venetian richness both in the columns of Sicilian jasper,
twenty in number, and in the carved ceiling of blue and
gold, with splendid escutcheons. Look for the Renaissance tomb of Archbishop Caprania in the left transept,
and in the right transept for the more modern tomb of
Leonardo Pesaro by Canova; also, in the sacristy, for a
lovely tabernacle by Mino da Fiesole. Relics of St.
Mark the Evangelist and also of St. Mark the Pope (335-

336) are preserved beneath the high altar, and a finger of St. Patrick has found its way here. You can think of St. Dominic, a less legendary figure, as preaching here, to crowded congregations, in the thirteenth century.

Following the Via del Plebiscito by the north wall of the Palazzo Venezia, we come to the Corso Vittorio Emmanuele II, and are at once at the Gesù, the great florid church on the left, sumptuous both without and within. It is here, in the left transept, under conditions of august pomp, that the remains of St. Ignatius Loyola, the founder of the Jesuits, repose. Of this remarkable man a few words must be said. His name was Inigo Lopez de Ricalde and he was born in 1491, the name Loyola coming from the Spanish castle and estates belonging to the family. Until he was thirty, Inigo was a soldier; then, during the siege of Pampelune, by André de Foix, he was shot through the legs and his life was despaired of. Recovering —although henceforward always lame—he became devout, and dedicated what might remain of his days to austerity and religion. At first he subjected himself to the rigours of monastic life, but realizing that he could be of more use in the world itself, he travelled to Jerusalem, to Spain, where he learned Latin, and was imprisoned and released, to Paris, on foot from Barcelona, to Belgium, and to London, always living on alms and always preaching. His gospel he had already outlined in his *Spiritual Exercises*, although that work was not completed till some years later.

It was in 1534 that Ignatius finally attached to himself, in Paris, the six friends who were to be the original upholders of the Jesuits, their first Mass being said in the church of St. Mary on Montmartre. Among them was François Xavier, whose altar is in the right transept of the Gesù.

In 1537 Ignatius was ordained priest; but not till

Christmas Day, 1538, did he say Mass in public, and then at S. Maria Maggiore in Rome. It was in 1537 that he had come to Rome, from Vicenza, seeing on the way the famous vision in which God set him at the side of Christ, and Christ uttered the words "I shall be propitious to you in Rome"; and once in Rome he and his friends toiled ceaselessly for the sick and poor of the city.

In 1540 the Pope, Paul III, conferred his sanction on the new Company, or Society, of Jesus. Ignatius Loyola died on July 31, 1556, and was canonized in 1628. If you would read the condensed story of his life and his effort, told with consummate skill and an almost lyrical passion, you will find it in Macaulay's essay on Von Ranke's *History of the Popes*.

Saint Ignatius' day, July 21, is one of moment at the Gesù. December 31 is also a great occasion. The singing is the best in Rome, and on Sunday mornings the church is crowded, partly for the music, and partly for the sermon.

I suppose that Rome has no church more suggestive of wealth and pomp. Indeed the bad taste into which its ecclesiastical decorators can too easily fall is only too evident. Loyola himself could hardly do anything but shudder at the loud extravagances of his shrine, with its flaunting bronze and precious stones, and his image life-size in silver. There is, however, a delicate little pulpit near the entrance, in white and coloured marble, that could not be more charming.

Rome has, not very distant from the Gesù, in the Piazza S. Ignazio off the Via del Caravita, another church dedicated to Loyola. The exterior of S. Ignazio gives little indication of its immensity within. You lift the padded screen of the door (never a small task for the aged and infirm) and are in what in England would be a cathedral, but here in Rome is merely one more church. Ignatius

Loyola is the Saint in chief, but St. Aloysius, his disciple, is most honoured here. The frescoes on the ceiling, a riot of angels, in full flight, can be seen rightly only from a point indicated by the sacristan, when the perspective is clear.

It was Pope Gregory XV (1621-1623), whose tomb is in this church, that canonized both Loyola and Francis Xavier. As a Pope his principal interest was in promoting the Church's missionary activities. He was buried in St. Peter's, but the remains were brought here by his nephew, Cardinal Ludovico Ludovisi, who built the church. On the roof is the time ball that gives the signal of noon to the gun on the Gianicolo.

Let me say here, in parenthesis, that perhaps the completest antidote to the ornateness of the Gesù and St. Ignatius which could be prescribed, is to be found in S. Giorgio in Velabro, the very early basilica which you find near the Palatine entrance in the Via S. Teodoro. Velabro means a marsh, this district being very low: indeed, you are shown a mark in the porch of the church indicating the height of a recent flood. This, one of the oldest churches in Rome, has been restored without any modern adulteration. The original windows with mica instead of glass remain, and the whole is beautifully soft and restful in hue. S. Giorgio is dedicated to our own patron saint, St. George, and it should therefore be of additional interest to English visitors, who will find no other Georgian shrine in Rome. His head, his spear and a portion of his standard once were here, but I cannot say if they still are. Giotto is said to have frescoed the apse but the present picture, in which we see St. George and Christ, is not his.

The Corso Vittorio Emmanuele II and its older dependencies contain many of Rome's finest palaces, but these palaces do not equal in architectural distinction those of

Florence, or in charm those of Venice. There is a bleak
austerity about them, and most have declined in rank.

The palace opposite the Gesù is the Altieri. The fluent
hand of the painter Carlo Maratta, so attractive to seven-
teenth-century Romans, will be found here. In fact, his
paintings are everywhere in the city and I might have
pointed them out both in S. Marco and in the Gesù, but
did not.

The next great church on the left is S. Andrea della
Valle, another florid fane, made important by the Strozzi
chapel, designed by Michael Angelo, and by Domenichino's frescoes of scenes in the life of St. Andrew.

The palace on the other side of the road is the Massimo
alle Colonne, designed by Peruzzi, a very attractive building. In the adjoining palace, the Pierro, the press was
set up in which were prepared the first printed books that
Rome produced. The adjoining church is S. Pantaleo,
and the large severe palace on the piazza is the Braschi,
notable for its staircase. It is now the Ministry of the
Interior, and if you walk round the left side, you will
come, at the corner at the back, on the Piazza di Pasquino, to a battered shapeless figure against the side.
This is the famous Pasquino, a relic of a classical group,
which, on St. Martin's day every year in the sixteenth
century and onwards, was the recipient of satirical verses,
the writers of which delivered their minds on the short-
comings of others, usually of those in authority, or of the
Pope. The earliest of these squibs are said to have been
the work of one Pasquino, a schoolmaster, cobbler, or
tailor (opinions vary), living close by, whose name in
course of time came to be used as a description of such
literature—pasquinade.

The replies to the Pasquino attacks were deposited on a
gigantic statue of a river-god which had been found in
the Campus Martius and set up in the street called after

it, the Via di Marforio. Pasquino attacked and Marforio repulsed, often in the form of written dialogues.

All that, however, is now over; the newspaper has arrived to take the place of both, and Pasquino, all neglected, is here, while the Marforio has been moved to the courtyard of the Capitoline Museum.

If we were to continue for a minute behind the Palazzo Braschi, we should find ourselves in the very interesting Piazza Navona, or Circo Agonale, which was originally a stadium for chariot races, built by Domitian, but is now a poor people's open space and one of the refuges from the terrifying Roman motorist. Churches and small shops surround it, and in the middle are three fountains, two by Bernini. Of these the most ambitious is the Fontana del Quattro Fiumi, or Four Rivers, the four being the Ganges, the Nile, the Danube and—no, not the Rhine, the Seine, the Tiber or the Thames, but the Rio de la Plata. This fountain gives us Bernini in his most joyous and fecund mood. The figures of the rivers are great gay old fellows, and there is a cheerful splashing always in the air. Above them rises an obelisk originally erected in honour of Domitian, then moved to the Circus of Maxentius and now established here. Bernini's other fountain is that to which, arriving from the Corso Vittorio Emmanuele II, we come first: the Moro, with its many Tritons. At the other end is a modern fountain, dating only from 1878, in which sea-horses and naiads frolic. There is a lamentable tendency to be frugal with the water supply, and the little Navonese have a rather ugly habit of throwing things into the basins. With a richer flow and constant cleaning, these fountains would make the Piazza Navona one of the pleasantest spots in Rome.

It is at its liveliest during the fair called La Befana, which begins on the feast of the Epiphany, when tin

THE TEMPLE OF VESTA WITH THE CHURCH OF
S. MARIA EGIZIACA BEHIND IT

[*See page* 133

trumpets are sold in their thousands for every boy to blow.

The two churches in the Piazza Navona are, on the east side, S. Giacomo de' Spagnuoli, and on the west, S. Agnese. San Giacomo, or St. James of Compostella, was built in the twelfth century for the Spaniards in Rome; S. Agnese stands on the site of St. Agnes's martyrdom and the little chapel erected over it. St. Agnes, a child of thirteen, was put to death in 305, under Domitian, for refusing to officiate at the altar of Minerva. For this offence she was condemned to be burnt alive; but the flames parted and refused to harm her. She was then decapitated. While in her prison, which is supposed to have been the present vault of the church, she was attended by an angel who communicated to her such radiance that those who looked were almost blinded. A son of the Prefect, coming to jeer at her, was actually blinded; but, on the intercession of St. Agnes, was healed and became a Christian. St. Agnes, whose day, January 21, is of great importance in Rome, is the special patroness of chastity. After her death she is said to have visited her parents with a lamb—hence the presence of the lamb in so many pictures of her, typifying her as the bride of Christ. To many of us she is best known through the superstition that makes the story of Keats's poem "The Eve of St. Agnes."

An historical relic of great interest in the church is the altar, two of whose columns, of *verde antico*, were once part of the arch of Marcus Aurelius in the Corso, which Pope Alexander VII removed. Velasquez's Pope Innocent X is buried here.

Just behind S. Agnese are two other churches of importance—S. Maria della Pace, of which I speak in Chapter IX, and S. Maria dell' Anima, St. Mary of the Holy Souls, a title drawn from the marble group in the tym-

panum, and emphasized in a painting by Giulio Romano
over the high altar. It is now the church of the German
students, whose hospice is next door and whose scarlet
robes are continually to be seen brightening the neighbourhood. Pope Adrian VI, the simple Utrecht cleric
who succeeded the sophisticated and complex Leo X and
found his post too onerous, is buried here.

Returning to the Corso Vittorio Emmanuele II we
come quickly to the huge and beautiful Palazzo della Cancelleria, a perfect example of Renaissance architecture.
After a long and mixed historical career, the Palace,
which belongs to the Papacy, is now the seat of the
Academy of Christian Archæology. Frescoes by Vasari,
the biographer of the great painters, will be found here.
You should look into the court for its double row of
arches, grey and graceful. The adjoining church is S.
Lorenzo in Damaso, with a simple and distinguished
tomb in the left aisle and a mass of negligible modern
frescoes.

Turning down the side street by the Cancelleria, you
come to the Piazza Campo di Fiore, where there is a
small flower-market, but no better than the Spagna steps
—indeed, Rome has flower-stalls everywhere. In the
midst is a statue of Giordano Bruno, who was tried for
heresy in 1600, and burnt on this actual spot. The
scene of an earlier tragedy lies hereabouts too, for Pompey's theatre covered much of the neighbouring ground
and it was in the Porticus Pompeiana that in 44 B. C.
Julius Cæsar was assassinated.

The most imposing of all the private palaces of Rome
is a few yards away—the Palazzo Farnese, begun by
Antonio Sangallo the younger, continued by Michael
Angelo and completed by Giacomo della Porta, the same
three architects who brought Bramante's dome of St.
Peter's to perfection. The pedimented windows to which

PALAZZO VENEZIA TO THE TIBER

Michael Angelo was so partial are here to be seen at their best in the stern gravity of the courtyard, and contrasting with the massive arches. Note the rich but delicate ornamentation of the barrelled ceiling of the entrance. The *loggia* on the Tiber side of the palace is by Giovanni della Porta. Raphael's pupils, the brothers Caracci, painted the frescoes here, all mythological subjects. The palace is now the French Embassy and Consulate, and the French School of History and Archæology has its headquarters here.

Resuming our walk along the Corso Vittorio Emmanuele we find on our right the Chiesa Nuova, in which a great northern artist disports himself, no less than Rubens, who was in Rome soon after the church was finished.

The pretty little building on the left just before we reach the bridge is a museum of Egyptian and classical sculpture left to the city in 1905 by Baron Giovanni Barracco. To give Rome, which has so much classical sculpture that is perfect and unrivalled—at the Vatican, at the Capitol, at the Baths of Diocletian and elsewhere —a little collection of antiques, almost all fragmentary, was a bold deed. But since one taste controlled the assembling of these objects, whereas those other great collections lack any such individuality, this little museum has a character of its own and should not be disdained. Perhaps the "Cagna ferita"—a bitch licking a wound— is the most famous of its treasures; but there are some beautiful heads of women, and among others an old man (No. 143) and the infant Nero, a child pure as dew.

At the end of the Corso we come to Rome's latest and most splendid bridge, named after the same monarch, which takes us straight to St. Peter's. From this bridge, with its pompous emblematic groups, the Tiber is not less disappointing than anywhere else. No historic stream, at any rate in its city life, has so little beauty or romance.

Had we turned to the left from the Corso Vittorio Emmanuele II down the wide and busy Via Torre Argentina, becoming in time the Via Arenula, we should have seen Rome at almost its least ancient, and have crossed the Tiber by the Ponte Garibaldi; first, however, seeking out the Piazza Mattei, partly for the collection of ancient reliefs that have been built into its walls, but chiefly for the Fontana delle Tartarughe, or Tortoises, which some people think Rome's most attractive fountain.

If, however, finding so much bustle distasteful, instead of crossing the Tiber we followed its bank to the left, we should correct this modernity when we came, behind the Synagogue, to early Rome again, in the shape of the Portico of Octavia. This gateway was erected by Augustus in honour of his sister, as the entrance to the great enclosure in which stood temples to Jupiter and Juno. Very sacred ground. The Theatre of Marcellus, just beyond, begun by Julius Cæsar and finished by Augustus, was named after Octavia's son.

I went out of my way, a little while ago, to refer to the primitive simplicity of S. Giorgio in Velabro. This would be the time to visit it, for it is only a little way behind the theatre. Adjoining the church is an arch, which the money-changers and silversmiths who had their offices in the adjacent Forum Boarium in the days of Septimius Severus (193-202), erected in honour of that Emperor. The Forum Boarium, or cattle-market, extended from the curious archway just here to the river. The history of the arch is not clear; it is known as the Janus Quadrifrons and may have been raised in honour of Constantine the Great. The four sides face the points of the compass. The attendant who shows the arch of Septimius Severus also has the key of the alley leading to the Cloaca Maxima, or main drain of the Forum. There is no need to see this, but the moss-covered walls have a curious sombre quality, and a Piranesi or Méryon would find a subject to his hand.

Another church in this neighbourhood, of a similar, althovgh not quite so perfect, simplicity as S. Giorgio in Velabro, is S. Maria in Cosmedin, which has some of the richest old mosaic in Rome and the purplest porphyry. These mosaic pavements of Rome were often the gift of wealthy patrons of the Church; but they were also often paid for by humbler devotees, each contributing a square foot. The little church was built in the sixth century on the foundations of a temple of Ceres. Like S. Clemente, S. Maria has a little enclosed choir of white marble with white marble ambones and some pretty mosaic pattern in colour and gold. In the crypt are the remains of many martyrs.

The great stone mask in the end wall of the vestibule is known as the Bocca della Verità, from the circumstance that if you place your hand in the mouth while telling a lie, it will bite you. I have not tried it.

Opposite S. Maria in Cosmedin is one of the most charming buildings in Rome—known as the Temple of Vesta, but really the shrine of Mater Matuta, the goddess of the dawn, and also a friend to those that go down to the sea in ships. When it was built the Tiber was navigable. The removal of the inner building would make these lovely columns twice as lovely. The neighbouring square temple, also filled in, was built in the sixth century B.C. as a temple of Fortune. In the ninth century A.D. it became a Christian church.

CHAPTER XIII

Trastevere and the Janiculum Hill

The Ship-shaped Island—A Poet in a tall Hat—Callixtus I—
S. Maria in Trastevere—St. Cecilia and her Martyrdom—A House
beneath a Church—The Farnesina Palace—Raphael's mythological
Fancies—S. Pietro in Montorio—Bramante's Temple—Garibaldi
and his Red-Shirts—The great Patriot Hero—The View from the
Janiculum—The Lighthouse without an Ocean—Torquato Tasso.

IF we cross to Trastevere, Rome's Surrey side, by the
bridge near those two temples, we have on our right
the ruins of the Ponte Rotto, so called because it was
broken in a flood in 1598, but known for centuries before
as the Pons Æmilius, dating from 181 B.C. The island
beyond it, with its houses and church, the Isola Tiberina,
was once the shrine of Æsculapius, one of whose serpents,
in 291 B.C., delivered Rome from the plague. That is
the story, which might be tried on the Bocca della Verità.
You will notice that the island is shaped like a ship.

Entering Trastevere by its main road we come at once
on the left to the statue of an agreeable fellow in a top
hat. This engaging Bohemian, in life, was Giuseppe
Gioachino Belli, a satirical sonnetteer of the first half of
the nineteenth century.

The cathedral of this district is S. Maria in Trastevere, which claims to be descended from the earliest
church, or, at any rate, earliest public meeting-place, of
Christians in Rome. The builder was Callixtus I
(217-222), the fifteenth Pope after St. Peter to hold office,
and, like St. Peter, a martyr. Before he became Pope he
was the caretaker of the Appian Way catacombs that

134

now bear his name; and his body is under the high altar of this church, which was built by Innocent II in the twelfth century. You see, in the mosaics in the apse, the figures both of Callixtus and of Innocent (who is carrying a model of the church).

S. Maria in Trastevere may be the Cathedral, but the principal church of Trastevere for the tourist is that of St. Cecilia, whose statue in death, by Maderna, is to be seen in plastic reproductions and photographs in all the souvenir shops. The legend has it that Cecilia was a patrician girl of the third century with a Christian mother and pagan father. Although vowed to virginity, she was given by her father to a pagan wooer, Valerian, who, with the aid of an angel visitant, was converted, and soon after, together with Cecilia's two brothers, was put to death. Cecilia was condemned to be suffocated by steam. After surviving many hours' exposure unhurt, she was sentenced to decapitation. Three times did the axe fall, making deep gashes, but could not sever the neck. The victim lived on for three days and then with her last breath expressed the wish that upon her house a church should be built. This is the church, often restored, which claims to incorporate the actual *caldarium* containing the steam for her torture.

That was in the third century. We now come to more modern times. In 1599 the tomb of St. Cecilia was opened and the body found to be as in life, without a sign of decay. For several weeks the devout flocked to see it, and the ruling Pope, Clement VIII, commanded Maderna to make the statue, which is an exact copy of the saint's exhumed form. The church has pictures by both Guido Reni and Domenichino celebrating the Saint, and there is a fine wall tomb near the door; but otherwise it is of no interest. Beneath it, however, you find traces of St. Cecilia's parents' house, which is in good preservation, although not so remarkable as that under SS. Giovanni e Paolo.

The other important Trastevere attraction to strangers is the Farnesina Villa, where Raphael, whom we have already seen as a religious painter, is to be found engaged upon mythological fantasies. Here he is at his gayest. The theme of the principal scenes is the story of Psyche, and her persecution by Venus through jealousy excited by her beauty. These are in the principal room, which was originally a garden room, almost a loggia, but now has windows. Considering that the weather once penetrated here, the condition of the frescoes is amazing. It will be remembered that Cupid, Venus's son, who is really the central figure and hero of the series, declined to support his mother in her feud. The fresco (No. 2) in which the God of love calls the attention of the Three Graces to the charms of Psyche is the freshest of all. Mercury starting on his quest of Psyche, and Cupid receiving Jupiter's kiss and blessing, are among my favourites. The designs alone were Raphael's; his pupils coloured them: among those pupils, as their assistant, being the young Domenichino. But the main pictures are not all; the details, the floral borders and the subsidiary scenes are the perfection of joyous wall painting.

In the next room we find Raphael both as designer and painter, in the beautiful scene of Galatea crossing the ocean, with all her attendants about her. Just as a modern monarch entering harbour is accompanied by cruisers and destroyers, while above him aeroplanes manœuvre in the air, so is Galatea surrounded by her Tritons and water nymphs, and in the sky by her attendant Loves with bows and arrows.

We will now climb the Gianicolo or Janiculum hill.

S. Pietro in Montorio, which calls for stout legs and unusual devoutness on the part of the poor who worship

THE CASTEL SANT' ANGELO AND THE PONTE SANT' ANGELO
[*See page* 140

there, is at the top of a hill of unusual length and steepness, and was built on the spot which tradition assigns to St. Peter's martyrdom, as we saw it depicted by Giotto in the sacristy of that Saint's largest church. The exact situation of the cross to which he was nailed is pointed out in one of the chapels, by the sacristan, but Bramante's circular temple, in the courtyard, is also said to cover the same historic position. As for that exquisite structure, it is as important for some of the surrounding buildings to be removed from it as for the internal structure in the Temple of Vesta to be cleared away. The grave of Beatrice Cenci is said to be in front of the high altar of this church.

From the terrace you get one of the finest views of Rome, and behind it is the glorious fountain of Paul V, the best Roman fountain in the cataract manner, after the Trevi.

The Janiculum hill, where, at noon, the gun is fired which sets all Rome looking at its watch, has, like the Pincio, its public gardens with a view—the Passeggiata Margherita—and also its Valhalla. On the Pincio we saw the busts of all the great Italians and in a loggia the equestrian statue of Vittorio Emmanuele II. On the Janiculum we find a colossal and magnificent equestrian statue of Garibaldi, set at a most imposing height, and busts of his principal followers all about it. The Colleoni in Venice must always be the first equestrian statue in the world, but the daring altitude at which the sculptor of the Garibaldi placed his hero makes it thrilling and unforgettable. A "horseman in the sky" indeed.

A word here as to Garibaldi, but for whom Rome to-day would be a very different city. Born in 1807, he was brought up as a sailor. When a young man he plotted with Mazzini, was caught and sentenced to death, but escaped to South America, where for several years he was a freebooter in various wars, and so successful as the head of an Italian legion in Uruguay that he received his pardon and was able to return to Italy. Rome, then a republic, made him general of its forces, and for the next few years he was fighting against the French, the Neapolitans, the Spanish and the Austrians. It was while he was trying to drive the Austrians from Venetian soil that he met with his most serious reverse, and during his flight his devoted wife, Anita, died. Escaping to America, he made a small fortune with a trading vessel and was able to return to Italy in 1854 and to build a home on the island of Caprera.

He might now have rested, but the cause of United Italy was too strong and he again took the field. His greatest triumph was the capture of Sicily and election as "Dictator"; his next, the conquest of Naples, with his red-shirts, into which city his King, Vittorio Emmanuel II, not always too well pleased with such a firebrand lieutenant, entered in state in 1860, Garibaldi effacing himself with perfect modesty.

The rest of his life was a series of splendid military efforts rather than successes, his impetuosity and impatience being not always the best equipment for a commander. In 1864 he was given the freedom of the City of London, amid scenes of frantic enthusiasm, for he was our hero too, and we named a blouse and a biscuit after him; in 1870 he fought with the French against the Prussians. Later, he took an active part in Italian politics. When, in 1882, he died, the whole world wept.

The view from the Janiculum is as spacious as that from the Pincio, but is not so fine. Seen from the east Rome is more impressive than (as here) from the west. Moreover, looking east, you do not see St. Peter's, which is round the corner in the north. The lighthouse, so oddly placed here, was the gift of the Argentines in Rome. By day it has no particular function to fulfil, and is not beautiful, but all through the night it flashes the Italian colours for the city to see.

Driving from this pharos in the direction of St. Peter's, we come to the little church of S. Onuphrius, famous in literature as being the home of the poet Torquato Tasso, who had his rooms in the cloisters and left his name to a little museum here. His tomb (he died in 1595) is in the first chapel on the left. The frescoes outside, under glass, by Domenichino, illustrate the life of St. Jerome.

Another likeness between the Janiculum and the Pincio may be mentioned here. You remember Corot's basin under the ilexes in front of the Villa Medici? Well, at S. Onuphrius, there is another basin under ilexes, and although no St. Peter's can be seen across it, not even San Carlo, there is a domed church conveniently placed.

CHAPTER XIV

The Castle of S. Angelo

The Bridge of S. Angelo—Bernini's Angels—The Emperor Hadrian—An Imperial Tomb—The missing Lift—Gregory the Great's Vision—The Archangel Michael—Engines of War—The Passage to the Vatican—Popes in Comfort—Benvenuto Cellini—The Siege of the Castle—An Escape from a Fortress.

HAD we left the Corso Vittorio Emmanuele II at the right, at the Via Banco di S. Spirito, we should have come to that older and more famous bridge, the Ponte di S. Angelo. The newest bridge, named after Vittorio Emmanuele II, was finished in 1911; this earlier one as long ago as 136, or at least the first bridge built here, upon which various structures have been imposed since, was then built. But on the way we should look at the Banco di S. Spirito itself, because of its association, as a tablet testifies, with Benvenuto Cellini, who worked there when it was the Papal Mint.

More of Cellini later; let us now cross the Ponte di S. Angelo, threading our way between Bernini's Angels of the Passion, and enter the Castel Sant' Angelo, which looms up so nobly at the far end.

When I say that Rome has no more arresting building than this, I am not making an exception even of St. Peter's or of the Colosseum. St. Peter's is more beautiful; the Colosseum is more imposing. But we have seen domes before, and amphitheatres before; nowhere else that I can name is there a circular fortress like this, rising from the river, immense and solid, with a rich band of corbels all around it and a glorious archangel on the top.

140

THE CASTLE OF S. ANGELO

The Castel Sant' Angelo, begun by the Emperor Hadrian in the year A. D. 136, as the tomb of himself and his successors, was used as a royal mausoleum until the death of Caracalla in 217. Hadrian, who succeeded Trajan in 117, was one of the most enlightened of the emperors, a scholar, a poet, a statesman, a great traveller and a great builder. We see now his tomb and his bridge; we have seen the Pantheon; we shall in course of time visit his wonderful villa near Tivoli, which, though now in ruins, retains traces of every kind of luxury and splendour. Many of the works of sculpture now preserved in Rome were found there. Even more active as a builder was he in Athens than in Rome. His travels took him as far as Britain, in 122, where he built the famous rampart from the Tyne to the Solway—Hadrian's Wall. As a domestic statesman, one of the problems in Rome that engaged his attention was the congestion of traffic. It is still unsolved.

Hadrian was capricious, cruel and untrustworthy, but he governed well and was popular by reason of his bribes, as I have elsewhere told. Incapable of enduring the slightest opposition, he was merciless to adverse critics. Apollodorus of Damascus, for example, the architect of Trajan's forum, was banished for daring to find fault with one of the Emperor's plans. On the other hand, Favorinus the sophist agreed with him even when he was obviously in error, excusing himself by the remark that it was unwise to differ from the master of thirty legions.

The tour of the Castello is fatiguing by reason of the long, enclosed, and very steep spiral incline. There was once a lift, installed by Pope Julius II, but only its shaft remains. This surely, in our day, is a very odd anachronism when we remember that the campanile of St. Mark's in Venice had to fall down before a lift was added to it.

141

A WANDERER IN ROME

On entering you look first at the Castle's massive foundations, and then, in a little museum, at models and drawings of the tomb as it probably was before the claims of the dead gave way to the pressing needs of the living and the mausoleum became a fort, centuries before the Popes decided that here was their ideal bolt-hole. Upon the walls of the tomb was then a sloping garden of cypress, above all rising a golden gigantic figure of Hadrian. The models give him four golden horses, but these are an improbable accessory, because the quadriga is an emblem not of death but victory. The walls of the building were covered with marble, only a mere vestige of which may be seen to-day, and there were sixty-five marble statues, most of which were broken up later for ammunition. Two figures remain to give us an idea of the world's loss —the Dancing Faun in the Uffizi at Florence and the Drunken Faun at Munich. The giant pigna, or pine cone, in the Giardino della Pigna in the Vatican, is sometimes said to have come from Hadrian's tomb.

It was in the fifth century that the tomb was first adapted for a fortress; it was in 1395 that the Popes made it their own, holding it until 1870. Its present form dates from the reign of Pope Nicholas V (1447-1455), who brought Fra Angelico to Rome.

When the ashes of Hadrian and his family were removed, no one seems to know; but there is no trace of them now. You are shown the position of the central chamber where the urns rested, and no more.

The dominating statue of the Emperor must have gone early, because there can have been nothing there when, in the year 590, while Rome was being swept by the plague, Pope Gregory the Great, at the head of a procession on its way to the tomb of St. Peter, glancing up at the pagan mausoleum, saw, as in a vision, the Archangel Michael posed there in the act of sheathing his sword.

THE CASTLE OF S. ANGELO

This the pontiff knew to be a sign that the scourge was over; and in recognition the mausoleum was Christianized. A chapel was built on its summit by Boniface IV and Sant' Angelo became its name, although its function as a martial stronghold did not change.

At the British Museum is a Book of Hours, once belonging to the Sforza family, in which you will find a gaily illuminated picture of Pope Gregory the Great and all the procession on their knees looking upward in reverence at the celestial apparition. The architecture and topography suggest that the artist (unlike Mr. Morley) was never in Rome; but the right spirit is here.

The present figure of St. Michael (the angel in the clouds) dates from 1752, superseding that in marble by Montelupo, with iron wings, which we shall find in the Cortile delle Palle, or the courtyard of the cannon balls. The balls remain in symmetrical heaps, obsolete and inutile, a reminder of the enmity of war to art, for they were shaped from beautiful statues. In the garden of the Castello you may see a contemporary catapult, while in the adjacent military museum are many other relics of mediæval fighting.

The bellicose history of the Castello is too long and too monotonous to tell. Whatever party was in power in this city of strife made it their military headquarters, until, in 1379, it was almost destroyed. But under Boniface IX (1389-1404) it entered upon a new career as a private residence of the Popes, and also a very present help to Popes in times of trouble, although the passage from the Vatican seems to have been in existence long before that era. This passage, which is very like that one in Florence, which connects the Uffizi and the Pitti, you may trace most of the way to the Vatican, either from the street, or looking down from the Castello's height. You may even reconstruct the moments of the

Popes' arrival, either serene, bent upon a pleasant retired evening, or in terror.

The restorers of the Castello, while retaining its strength, made it very habitable, with banqueting rooms, an outdoor theatre, and even dungeons and oubliettes for awkward customers. Paul II (1464-1471) held a review of the papal army here, in 1471, as an object-lesson to Borso d'Este. The secret passage was put into new repair by Alexander VI the Borgia Pope (1492-1503), who added to the comfort and splendour of the private apartments, even to the extent of employing Pinturicchio to paint their walls. Julius II (1503-1513) spent much time here, and remained here when Charles VIII of France entered Rome in 1494. The pretty little loggia over-looking the bridge and the city was Julius's addition; but not yet were Bernini's angels in existence. The Medici Pope who followed Julius, Leo X (1513-1521), often made his home here too. Many were the receptions, pomps and entertainments of those days. But in the reign of the next Medici Pope, Clement VII (1523-1534) for whom Michael Angelo is said to have designed the little chapel in the Cortile delle Palle, and who was the first Pope to instal a bathroom, came more bloodshed, for the Castello was the very centre of the fighting when the troops of the Emperor Charles V, under the Constable of Bourbon, besieged the city, conquered it and laid it waste. Never was Rome the same again. But of the misfortunes of Rome under Clement VII I speak else-where.

It is now, under the shadow of this tragedy, that we rejoin Benvenuto Cellini, goldsmith, sculptor, adven-turer, probably liar, and servant of Clement VII.

Benvenuto Cellini was a Florentine, born in 1500, and it is at Florence, in the Loggia dei Lanzi and the Bar-gello, that his masterpieces are found. It has been sug-

144

THE PERSIAN SIBYL
  After the fresco by MICHAEL ANGELO *in the* Sistine Chapel

[*See page* 108

JOVE AND CUPID
After the fresco by RAPHAEL *in the Villa Farnesina*

[*See page* 136

gested that the face discernible at the back of the head
of his Perseus in the Loggia is a self-portrait. After
a stormy boyhood, which included banishment from
Florence, he became a goldsmith, and at nineteen he
reached Rome. Here he attracted the attention of Pope
Clement VII both as an artificer and musician.

In the year 1527, when Charles V's mercenaries descended on Rome, Benvenuto ceased to be a goldsmith
and became a soldier, and, if the Memoirs are to be believed, but for his presence in the Castello the fall of
Rome would have been greatly accelerated. "Never,"
he writes, "a day passed but I killed some of the be-
siegers. Once when the Pope was walking round the keep,
he saw a Spanish colonel in the Prati, whom by certain
signs he recognized; for the man had once been in his
service. While he watched he talked about him. I, who
was alone in the Angel, and knew nothing of what was
going on, nevertheless saw a man occupied about the
trenches. He had a little javelin in his hand, and his
dress was all of rose colour. Bethinking myself what I
could do against him, I took one of the gerfalcons that
I had there, a piece bigger and longer than a sacro, and
very like a small culverin. First I emptied it, and then
loaded it with a good quantity of fine powder mixed with
coarse. Then I aimed well at the red man, raising the
muzzle tremendously, for he was far away, and guns of
this sort cannot be expected to carry with precision at
that range. When I fired, I aimed exactly at the red
man's middle. He had slung his sword in front, in arrogant Spanish fashion, and my ball hitting his blade, the
man fell, cut in two. The Pope, who was looking for
nothing of the kind, was greatly pleased and astonished,
for it seemed impossible to him a gun should have so
long a range; nor could he understand how the man
should have been cut in half. Sending for me, he asked

me to explain. So I told him what ingenuity I had used; but as for cutting the man in two, it was a thing neither of us could get to the bottom of.

"Then, kneeling down, I begged him to remove from me the curse of this homicide, and of others I had committed in that castle in the service of the Church. Whereupon the Pope, raising his hands, made the sign of the cross broadly over my face, gave me his blessing and his pardon for all the homicides I had committed, or ever should commit, in the service of the Church Apostolic. So I left him, and once on the tower again I went on firing without stop, and hardly ever was shot of mine in vain. My drawing, my fine studies and my skill in music were all drowned in the roar of those guns; and were I to tell minutely all the fine things which I did in that infernally cruel business, I should strike the world with wonder.

"But not to be too lengthy, I shall pass them all over, save just a few of the most notable which I am forced to tell. So here I kept thinking day and night how best I could do my part in the defence of the Church. Now I knew that when the enemy changed guard, they passed through the big gate of Santo Spirito, which was within a moderate range. So I began to fire in that direction. But as I had to fire obliquely, I did not do all the mischief I should have liked, though every day my slaughter was considerable. Then the enemy, seeing their passage hindered, one night piled up more than thirty barrels on the crest of a roof, thus blocking my view. Considering the matter rather more carefully than I had done before, I turned all my five pieces of artillery right on the barrels, and waited till two hours before sunset, when the guards would be changed. Now, thinking themselves secure, they came along more slowly and in a denser mass than had been their wont; so, when I fired, I not only knocked down the barrels in my way, but killed more than thirty men in that one blast. This I repeated twice again, and threw the soldiers into great disorder; and the incident, joined to the fact that they had stuffed themselves with loot from their great sack, and were longing to enjoy the fruits of their labours, was the cause of their threatening to revolt and to desert."

Cellini claims to have fired the gun that killed the Constable of Bourbon; but it was a hollow achievement, for his death only infuriated his soldiers to greater efforts.

The same Castello which was the scene of Cellini's triumphs was later his prison—for he was always in trouble. The story of his evasion is one of the choicest passages in his book. "From that moment," he says, "I set to thinking about the best means of escape. As soon as they had shut the door on me, I went about examining the prison where I lay. When I believed I had certainly found a way of getting out, I began to devise a means of climbing down from the high castle keep. Then I took those new sheets of mine, which, as I have already said, I had torn into strips and well sewn together, and calculated what length would serve me to climb down by. When I had made up my mind about this, and prepared everything, I laid my hands on a pair of pincers, which I had stolen from a Savoyard warder of the castle. This man looked after the barrels and the cisterns; and he also worked at carpentering for his pleasure. Now he had several pincers and among them some huge solid ones. Just my affair, I thought; and I stole them, and hid them in my mattress. Then the time came for me to use the tool, and I began to try the nails of the hinges. As the door was a double one, the riveting of the nails could not be seen, so that when I tried to draw one out it gave me the greatest trouble; but in the end I succeeded. When I had drawn out the first nail, I bethought me how I should contrive that this should not be seen. I managed it by mixing some little rusty iron filings with a little wax, getting just the very colour of those long nails I had taken out. With this I began carefully imitating the nails in the supports of the hinges; and by degrees made a waxen counterfeit for every one I drew out. I left the hinges still attached at top and bottom with some of the old nails, which, however, I only put back after they had been cut, and then only lightly, so that they just held the hinge-plates and no more.

"This business gave me a deal of trouble; for the castellan dreamt each night that I had escaped and every now and then he sent to have my prison examined. The man who came to investigate had a bum-bailiff's name, Bozza, and behaved as such. He always brought with him another fellow called Giovanni, surnamed Pedignone. He was a soldier, and Bozza was a menial. This Giovanni never once came to my prison without insulting me. He was from Prato, where he had been an apothecary. Every evening he examined the hinges and the whole prison very carefully; and I would say to him, 'Keep a good look-out on me, for I am going to slip through your hands for a certainty.' These words stirred up a furious hatred between him and me. So with the utmost care I hid up my implements, that is, the pincers, a large dagger, and other things pertaining to my plan, in my mattress, along with the strips I had made.

"As soon as daylight came I used to sweep my room; and though by nature I liked cleanliness, I kept my place in specially good order then. When I had done my sweeping, I arranged my bed beautifully, and laid flowers on it, which I had a certain Savoyard bring me almost every morning. This was the Savoyard who had charge of the barrels and cisterns, and who worked at carpenter-

ing for his pleasure. It was from him I stole the pincers
with which I picked out the nails from the hinge-plates.

"Now to return to what I was saying about my bed.
When Bozza and Pedignone came in, I told them they
were to keep at a due distance from it, that they might
not foul and spoil it. When sometimes, just to annoy
me, they would touch it lightly, I would cry to them, 'Oh,
you dirty cowards! I'll get hold of those swords of
yours, and serve you a turn that will astonish you! Do
you think yourselves good enough to touch the bed of a
man of my sort? No care for my own life shall hold me
back, for I am sure to take yours. So leave me alone
with my troubles and my tribulations, and don't add to
them; otherwise, I'll let you see what a desperate man
can do.' All this they told to the castellan. But he
expressly ordered them not to go near my bed, and to
come to me without their swords; for the rest, they were
to keep a sharp look-out on me.

"When I was thus sure about the bed, I thought I had
done everything, for therein lay what I needed most for
the business. One feast-night, when the castellan was
feeling very ill, and his humours were at their height, he
kept on saying that he was a bat; and if they heard that
Benvenuto had flown away, they were to let him go, for he
would overtake me, since at night time he could certainly
fly better than I. 'Benvenuto,' said he, 'is only a sham
bat, but I'm a real one. And since he's been given into
my keeping, leave the business to me, for I'll come up with
him.' He had been in this condition for several nights
and had tired out all his servants. And I heard about it
through different channels, but especially from the Savoyard, who was a friend of mine. This feast-day evening
I had made up my mind to escape at all hazards. First
I prayed most devoutly to God, entreating His Divine
Majesty to defend me, and aid me in my perilous enter-

prise. Then I prepared everything I needed for the business, working all through that night. When day was
but two hours off, I removed the hinges with the greatest
trouble. But the wooden frame and the bolt also resisted
so that I could not open the door, and had, therefore,
to cut the wood. At last I succeeded; and then carrying
the strips of linen, which I had rolled round two pieces
of wood like flax on a spindle, I made my way out towards
the privies of the keep. From inside I perceived two tiles
on the roof, and thus I could climb up at once with the
greatest ease. I was wearing at the time a white jerkin,
white hosen, and a pair of buskins, into which I thrust
my dagger. Taking one end of my linen rope, I tied it
in the form of a stirrup round a piece of antique tile that
was built into the wall, and which stuck out hardly the
length of four fingers.

"This done, I turned my face to God, and said, 'Oh
Lord, my God, defend my cause! for Thou knowest that
it is good; and that I help myself.' Then I let myself go
gently, and supporting myself by the strength of my
arms, I reached the bottom. The moon was not shining,
but the sky was clear and fair. When my feet were on
the ground, I regarded the great descent I had made so
bravely, and went off much heartened, for I thought I
was free. But it was not so; for on that side the castellan
had had two very high walls built enclosing a poultry-run.
This place was barred with great bolts on the other side.
When I saw my way thus stopped, I was much vexed;
but while walking to and fro, thinking what I should best
do, I fell up against a large beam which had been covered with straw. With great difficulty I set it up against
the wall. Then by force of arm I climbed up on it to the
top. But as the wall was pointed, I was not solidly
enough planted there to draw the pole up after me. So
I determined to use a piece of the second rope of linen,

as the other I had left hanging from the keep. Well, binding it fast to the beam, I climbed down by it on the other side. This was far from easy; I was quite worn out at the end; and besides I had galled the palms of my hands, so that they bled. I therefore stayed to rest a while.

"When I felt sufficiently recovered, I made my way to the last wall, which looks towards Prati. There I laid down my linen rope, intending to fix it to a battlement, and get down from the lesser heights as I had done from the greater. But just at that moment I discovered that behind me was one of the sentinels on duty. Seeing here a hindrance to my plans, and knowing my life in danger, I made up my mind boldly to face the guard, who, perceiving my resolute demeanour, and that I was coming towards him with a weapon in my hand, quickened his step, and made as if to keep out of my way. I had left my ropes some way off; now I quickly turned back for them, and though I saw another sentinel, yet he appeared unwilling to see me.

"When I had picked up my linen ropes, I tied them to the battlement, and let myself go, but either I thought that I had almost reached the ground, while I was still some distance off, and let go my hands and jumped; or else my hands were too feeble to keep up the effort. At all events I fell, and in falling, I struck the back of my head, and lay there unconscious more than an hour and a half, so far as I could judge. The day was about to break, and the fresh, cool air that comes before the rising of the sun brought me to my senses; but yet my wits were not quite clear, for I thought my head was cut off, and that I was in purgatory. Little by little my powers came back to me, and I saw that I was outside the castle, and had a sudden remembrance of all that I had done."

A WANDERER IN ROME

A visit to the Castle of S. Angelo with those passages in mind is far more interesting (even if they are not strictly true) than without them. In the cell in which Benvenuto is said to have been imprisoned, where you may stand awhile and stifle, is a shadowy figure on the wall, called a Christ, from his pencil. In the floor is an oubliette which the guide assures you led straight to the Tiber. These oubliettes are frequent; there are two in the banquet-hall. In the rooms where the oil supply was kept is a trap door down which, in moments of necessity, that fluid, boiled, could be poured.

Let me complete the outline of Cellini's career. Free at last from his prisons and exiles and provided with a pardon, he returned to Florence, where he became the desire of all millionaires who needed gold work, and he spent some time at the court of François I at Fontainebleau, where Diane de Poitiers then reigned. But his quick temper and indifference to the health of anyone who stood in his way brought him continually into disfavour and he was never long in one place or in one service. Late in life he composed his memoirs, which are excellent reading even though the salt-cellar (Cellini, by the way, made for Clement VII the best salt-cellar in the world) must stand conveniently at the reader's side. He died, still a bachelor, in 1571.

From the roof of the Castello you have an all-round view of the city; and the identification of towers, domes and buildings is from this point a good test of one's Roman knowledge. The royal palace is the least comely edifice. One of the recent additions to Rome is a War Memorial on the further embankment wall of the Tiber. Rome has a memorial for each district, but none so unexpectedly placed as this.

The new residential quarter behind the Castel Sant'

REMAINS OF THE TEMPLE OF SATURN, WITH THE ARCH OF
SEPTIMIUS SEVERUS, AND THE CHURCH OF
SS. MARTINA E LUCA

[*See page* 172

THE CASTLE OF S. ANGELO

Angelo and the Palace of Justice, called the Prati, which ends in a row of barracks, is uninteresting; and in order to build it many fine antiquities were destroyed, including Michael Angelo's wall.

Chapter XV

S. Maria Sopra Minerva, Two Medici Popes and a Saint

Leo X and his Reign—Virtuoso and Voluptuary—Clement VII and his Reign—Disasters for Rome and the Church—A Gothic Church—Michael Angelo's Risen Christ—Fra Angelico's Tomb—St. Catherine of Siena.

HAVING heard so much of Clement VII we might perhaps look into the church of S. Maria sopra Minerva on our way back from the Castel Sant' Angelo and see his tomb. Born in 1478, the illegitimate son of Giuliano de' Medici, brother of Lorenzo the Magnificent, he was left an orphan when his father was assassinated in the Duomo at Florence by the Pazzi conspirators in a plot whose principal object was to kill Lorenzo himself. The boy was adopted by Lorenzo and educated with his sons, the young Michael Angelo being also permitted to share their lessons. One of these sons, Giovanni, became Pope Leo X, who in course of time was to make Giulio a cardinal, and indeed, being himself an indolent voluptuary, to leave to him much of the business of the pontifical office.

Perhaps since cousin Leo was Clement VII's predecessor, I should deal with him first. Let me say then that this spiritual prince, born in 1475, and thus only three years older than Clement, had the most refined and cultured training that his powerful and enlightened father could obtain for him, always with an idea that he should enter the Church. He was in point of fact made a Car-

154

dinal at the early age of seventeen. During the exile of the Medici from Florence between 1494 and 1512, he had a somewhat broken career, but after the death of Julius II in 1513 he was elected Pope and settled down to dominion and ease. Although there was much disturbance during his reign—wars with the French, wars with the Turks—and although it was during his reign that an Augustinian monk named Martin Luther lodged his protest against the Pope's sale of indulgences, which in course of time led to the Protestant Reformation, he did not allow his personal comfort to be much affected. "Let us enjoy the Papacy since God has given it to us," he is reported to have said. We see him in Raphael's famous portrait in the Pitti, at Florence, fat, masterful and sensual. He was also so extravagant that it was necessary to borrow recklessly and even to sell Cardinals' hats to obtain new funds. He treated the sacred side of his office very lightly—so lightly indeed as to have a hunting-lodge, which St. Peter can never have done. On the other hand, he was a friend of learning and art. He was the devoted patron of Raphael, he employed Michael Angelo, he restored the University of Rome and saw that scholars did not starve.

Dying in 1521, Leo was succeeded by Adrian VI, and then in 1523 came Giulio de' Medici as Clement VII, his age then being forty-five. Leo X had not added to the power of the Church or to the peace of his country. Clement VII was destined to lose millions of Catholic subjects and to see Rome reduced to ruin and misery. Controlled by cunning and vacillation, he seems always to have been on the wrong side. When he came to the Papal throne the two great belligerents of Europe were Francis I of France and the Emperor Charles V, and he alternately supported and betrayed them. The most serious result of his treachery was the attack on Rome by the Constable

---

of Bourbon of which I have spoken, during which the Pope was a refugee in the Castel Sant' Angelo. Later came the *impasse* with Henry VIII over the divorce of Catherine of Aragon and that monarch's repudiation of Wolsey and Rome. It is probably true to say that the Church of Rome never recovered from this Pope.

Other Popes buried at S. Maria sopra Minerva are Paul IV (1555-1559), Urban VII (1590), and Benedict XIII (1724-1730). Paul was the Neapolitan Pope who founded the Theatine Order, the purpose of which was to promote piety by personal example and to confound heresies by preaching the true doctrine. As a ruler he was intolerant and bellicose, and his hatred of Spain poisoned his reign. Few occupants of St. Peter's chair were less popular and at his death his statue was destroyed by the people.

Urban VII reigned only for twelve days, and Benedict XIII's term of office was undistinguished.

The church of S. Maria sopra Minerva stands on the site of a temple to Minerva built by Pompey (106-48 B.C.) in honour of his victories in Asia. Until 1870 the Popes came here in state on every anniversary of the Feast of the Annunciation. Perhaps, if the decision not to leave the Vatican is revoked, they may do so again. I think this church is already one of the most beautiful and impressive in all Rome; and if the glass in the circular windows over the arches were worthy, it would be perfect. Perhaps the unusual sight of our familiar northern Gothic architecture may account a little for the affection in which I hold it; but its proportions are so fine and its workmanship so stable that even the most prejudiced admirer of Palladian and baroque design must be touched. Of all the churches of Rome it is, however, almost the darkest, so that if you would see the tombs, you must choose a sunny day and an early hour.

S. MARIA SOPRA MINERVA

Most visitors here are drawn by the fame of Michael Angelo's figure of Christ with the Cross, which stands to the left of the choir. The Christ, as the master represented Him, was to be Christ risen; hence the nudity of the figure. The bronze girdle was added later; while the bronze shoe was a precaution against the kisses of the devout on the marble. Another object of interest to students is the tomb, in the passage just beside the Christ, of another and earlier Florentine artist, the beloved Fra Angelico, who was bidden to Rome by Pope Nicholas V to decorate his chapel in the Vatican, and died, while engaged on that task, in 1455.

The illumined figure of St. Catherine of Siena under the high altar is here by virtue of the circumstance that the room in which her death occurred, in 1380, in the Via S. Chiara, was removed to the sacristy, where it is an object of pilgrimage. This was because S. Maria sopra Minerva is a Dominican church and St. Catherine one of the glories of St. Dominic's Order.

Of the six St. Catherines, St. Catherine of Alexandria (the St. Catherine of the wheel) is perhaps the most famous, but St. Catherine of Siena is the most interesting. Signorina Benincasa, as I suppose she was called before she took the veil, was born on Palm Sunday in 1348, the year when Siena was more than decimated by the plague. Catherine, who was a twin, was one of twenty-five children of a prosperous dyer, whose abode, except that it has become a place of pilgrimage and is no longer a dwelling-house, is very much as it was in his day, although so many years have passed. The rooms still contain certain authentic vestiges of the Saint, and much new matter bearing upon her life has been added, including a series of modern frescoes.

The little Catherine took very early to piety, when only seven vowing herself to virginity and the service of

Christ, and at sixteen she converted a room in the house into a cell and remained there for two or three years in a state of ecstasy. Upon her father's death, however, when she was twenty-one, she took a more worldly position and became known in Siena as a ministering angel and a mediator. She visited the sick fearlessly (no small thing in that city of epidemics) and she mended quarrels. Gradually her reputation as a worker of miracles spread, the culmination of her mystical power being her reception of the stigmata—a scene often painted: that is to say, during a period of intense spiritual rapture, she was conscious of wounds on her hands, feet and heart, precisely similar to those inflicted upon Christ on the Cross. That was in 1375, and it set the seal on her holiness and peculiar sanctity, at any rate among Dominicans. The Franciscans, whose Founder had been similarly privileged by Heaven, were less enthusiastic.

Meanwhile, on the mundane side, Catherine's power was also growing: for she was shrewd in judgment and ready of speech; and in the year following the "stigmata" she was selected to make her famous entry into papal politics, and by all the means at her disposal—correspondence, conversations and personal argument—to persuade Gregory XI to give up Avignon and return to Rome. This end she succeeded in achieving. In her letters much of the story can be read. She appears there as a woman of considerable knowledge of the world, and no little self-esteem, but lacking in tenderness.

It is at S. Domenico in Siena that the only authentic portrait of her is to be found: the work of Andrea Vanni, an early Sienese painter. In this portrait she holds a lily in one hand and gives the other to an adoring nun to be kissed. Her face is sad and austere, with a long straight nose, and a mouth with a slight droop at each side. She looks determined and melancholy, and more than the age

S. MARIA SOPRA MINERVA

at which she died, which was only thirty-two or thirty-three. The ordinary non-contemporary painter of scenes in her life continually disregards its brevity; I can recall several pictures where she is quite elderly; and I am sure that the popular idea of her is as a venerable dame.

Among the treasures of Santa Maria sopra Minerva, which on a fine morning should be sought for, are the chapel of St. Thomas Aquinas with Filippino Lippi's frescoes; the painting of the Annunciation in the fourth chapel of the right aisle; the head of Christ by Perugino in the third chapel of the left aisle; and the statue of St. Sebastian, also there, perhaps by Mino da Fiesole. Also several very impressive tombs. But nothing is more impressive, at dusk, than the bearded Dominican monks quietly moving about in their white habits with black coats. They are the Middle Ages.

CHAPTER XVI

The Capitoline Hill

A City of Hills—Carducci's Poem—Rienzi, the Last of the Trib-
unes—The Campidoglio—The Dying Gladiator—The Capitoline Venus
—The Thorn Extractor—The pious Æneas—Romulus and Remus—
The Roman Custodian—S. Maria in Araceli—The Historian Gibbon
—The Christmas Recitations—The Tarpeian Rock.

THE visitor to Rome very quickly realizes the truth
of the statement that the city is built on hills.
Seven is the accepted number, but there seem to be more
than that: seventy at least. Let us now climb the smallest
of them, but also the most famous: the Capitoline; and
on that hill let us visit a venerable church and two galleries of sculpture and painting.

I think we will take the church last, approaching it
from behind the Capitoline Museum, although, to the in-
trepid, that flight of steps, where beggars sleep in the
sun, and at Christmas time toys are sold, may present no
obstacle. There is, however, a winding road to the Campidoglio, for vehicles, although the conscientious will
make a point of either ascending or descending the main
steps, or rather slopes, once.

Those who know Italian should pause at the foot to
read the verses on the stone—from the pen of the poet
Carducci (1836-1907). For those who do not know
Italian (among whom I am chief) I may say that the
poem is a birthday ode to Rome. Even though the past
was more glorious than the present, says the poet, even
though no longer along the Sacred Way do the four

THE DYING GLADIATOR
After the Statue in the Capitoline Museum

Photograph by Brogi

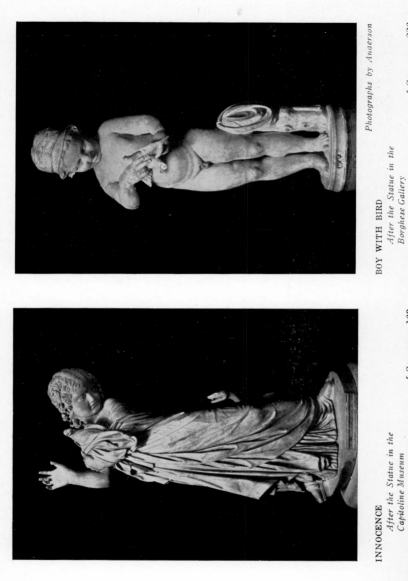

INNOCENCE
*After the Statue in the
Capitoline Museum*

[*See page* 163

BOY WITH BIRD
*After the Statue in the
Borghese Gallery*

Photographs by Anderson

[*See page* 226

white horses bend their necks for the triumph, whatever in the world to-day is civilized, great and august—that is still Roman. He who disdains Rome has a mind obscured by darkness and an evil heart in which sprout the weeds of barbarism. Finally the poet promises Rome new triumphs, not of Kings, not of Cæsars, not of chains binding human arms to ivory chariots, but triumph over the dark ages, over injustice.[1]

The statue near by, which many people take to be Savonarola, is really Bulwer Lytton's hero, Rienzi, the Last of the Tribunes. This ambitious man, Nicholas, or Cola, di Rienzo, was born in Rome in 1314, the son of a publican, and as a boy and youth was brought up in the country among peasants. At the age of twenty, returning to Rome—which was then in a very bad and lawless way, with the Popes in exile at Avignon—he took to history and spent all his time reading about the good old days and desiring their restoration. A gift of rhetorical eloquence, always attractive to the Romans, served him well, and in 1343 he became the mouthpiece of the Council of Thirteen on a mission to Pope Clement VI. Back in Rome again, Cola began to plot against the Roman nobility, and chiefly the powerful Colonna family, his aim being the creation of a new Republic with himself at the head. He wore either a toga or the ancient Roman armour, and, ceaseless in his oratory and promises of prosperity, actually succeeded in getting himself elected as Tribune, and his election approved by the Pope. He even struck his own coins. In his theatrical way he ruled wisely; but his head was not strong enough to prevent him from committing grandiose follies. After being baptized in Constantine's font at the Lateran, he had himself created a Knight with such subsidiary titles as "Friend of the Universe" and "Candidate of the Holy

[1] Rome's 2679th birthday was celebrated in 1926.

Ghost," and invited all the princes of the earth to assemble before him in Rome and do obeisance. Such conceit could not prosper, and after battle with the forces of the nobility whom he had humiliated, Rienzi, a physical coward, first took refuge in the Castel Sant' Angelo, repudiated by everybody, including the Pope, and then disappeared.

For several years he seems to have wandered about, but in 1534 was in Rome again, and again the darling of this fickle people, until he imposed another unpopular tax (his first had been the tax on salt, which led in part to his downfall), when they rose and, calling him "Traitor," burned his palace and stabbed him to death. His body, after hanging in public for two days, was cremated at the Castel Sant' Angelo.

In the cages at the top of the steps, on the left, should be eagles and wolves, the eagles of Rome, and wolves the descendants of the foster-mother of Romulus and Remus. It is a little odd that one finds so seldom in Rome the symbol of its origin; whereas in Siena, which claims Romulus's brother as a founder, the wolf and the little sucking boys are everywhere.

The Piazza del Campidoglio, which we now enter, was designed by Michael Angelo, but most of it was carried out by successors. The pedestal of the equestrian statue of Marcus Aurelius is his, and was set in position under his sorrowful eye. The statue, when it occupied its old place at the Lateran, was gilded. For centuries it was believed to be the Emperor Constantine. At one of Rienzi's banquets wine gushed from its mouth.

As you stand at the top of the steps, facing the famous Stoic Emperor, the building on the left is the Capitoline Museum, where the statue of the "Dying Gladiator" is; the building on the right is the Palace of the Conservatori, where the statue of the "Thorn Extractor" is; and the building in front of you is the Palazzo del Senatore, with a flight of steps designed by Michael Angelo. On the balustrade beside you are old Roman milestones, and the giant equestrians are supposed to be Castor and Pollux from the Theatre of Balbus.

The river-god facing you in the courtyard of the Capitoline Museum is the Marforio, of which I say something in connexion with Pasquino in another chapter.

The principal treasures of the Capitoline Museum have been so often reproduced, both in plaster casts and in photographs, that even a stranger from the wildest and woolliest west might have the feeling that he had been there before. My own steps take me first and last to the Marble Faun of Praxiteles, for although this is only a copy from the original at the Villa d'Este, it seems to have an ease and grace that could not be surpassed; but I suppose that the most powerful attraction here is the Dying Gladiator. The statue was discovered in the sixteenth century, and was probably part of a series of which the Gaul and his wife, to be seen at the Museum of the Terme, formed a part. The Dying Gladiator, sometimes called the Dying Gaul, is said to have been restored here and there by Michael Angelo.

Among the other famous sculptures of the Capitol (some of them reproduced in this book) are the little girl and the snake, called "Innocence," the Apollo, the Young Bacchus in basalt, the Young and Old Centaur in basalt, the Satyr between them in *rosso antico*, with his grapes and his goat; the Elder Agrippina; the Cupid and Psyche in their eternal kiss; the Venus of the Capitol; and the many heads of Cæsars and Roman citizens, one of Cicero being like a composite portrait of all America's lawyers.

The Capitoline Venus has not the charm of the Venus of Cyrene at the Terme of Diocletian; but it is a lovely

A WANDERER IN ROME

statue, unmistakably Greek and loveliest when seen from the back, turning its head to the left.

Across the road is the Palace of the Conservatori where more sculpture, pottery, and so forth, revealed by modern Roman excavations, is preserved, and where also is a series of splendid historical apartments. The most famous possession is the bronze figure of the boy removing a thorn from his foot, attributed to Myron the Greek. Look also for the head of Medusa by Bernini and a melancholy bust of Michael Angelo. Velasquez's Pope Innocent X, also in bronze, has a new magnificence.

The Capitoline Wolf, a blend of ancient and modern art, is also here. The twins may be a Renaissance addition, but as long ago as the year 65 B.C. the wolf was a sacred figure in the adjacent temple on whose ruins the church of the Aracœli now stands. Since the story of the foundation of Rome should be told somewhere in this book, let it be told in this room, although it might also, almost as fittingly, be related in the chapter on the Villa Umberto I, before Bernini's group of the Pious Æneas, for it was the pious Æneas who was, in a way, Rome's true begetter.

Thus. Some twelve centuries before Christ, after the fall of Troy, Æneas, carrying his father and his household gods and leading his son, Ascanius, fled, ultimately reaching Italy, where he made friends with the King of Latium and married his daughter Lavina. Coming in time to be himself king, he called his capital Lavinium, a town on the Tiber which afterwards became sacred in Roman eyes. The boy Ascanius, grown up, established himself at Alba Longa, in the Alban mountains, and was the first of a long line of kings.

In course of centuries the throne was occupied by Numita, who had a son, and a daughter, Rhea Silvia. He also had a jealous brother Amulius, who wanted to be king. This brother did not dare to kill Numita, but struck

164

at the succession by killing the son and persuading the daughter to become a Vestal Virgin. The gods, however, dispose. Anchises, it must be remembered, had been the son of Venus; it was Mars who now stepped in, with the result that Rhea gave birth to twins.

Amulius took instant action. He demanded that Rhea should be buried alive (a fate which Vestal Virgins who broke their vows had to expect) and he launched the two infants (whose names were Romulus and Remus) in a cradle on the foaming Tiber. It was not for nothing, however, that they had the divine Mars for a father. That god saw that the river bore them safely to a spot under the Palatine hill, and there they were found by a she-wolf, which (as you see) nourished them until a shepherd came on the scene and took them to his home. It was then only a matter of a few years for Romulus to build Rome and give it his name.

Upstairs are terra-cotta figures and vessels in profusion, and the giant figure of Hercules in gilded bronze excavated from the Forum Boarium, or cattle-market.

The picture gallery, founded by Benedict XIV (1740-1758), has a few notable works, but very few. Rubens's characteristic treatment of Romulus and Remus at lunch receives most attention: no contrast could be more sharp than that between the boy-cubs of the piece of statuary and the two voluptuous and massive infant gastronomes rioting near their foster-mother in this picture by the Flemish master. The self-portrait of Velasquez has a grave dignity, and Van Dyck's representation of the two courtly English poets, Killigrew and Carew, should not be missed. Nor should a Parmigianino. The classic fiddler in fresco in the first room is not Nero, but a figure in the story of Cupid and Psyche, by Annibale Caracci. Perhaps the most charming picture in the whole palace is the altar-piece in the little chapel downstairs, by Andrea d'Assisi.

The disproportionate figure above the fountain of the Palazzo del Senatore represents the spirit of Rome. Michael Angelo's intention was to place here a colossal Jupiter. From the roof a spacious view of Rome is obtained, far and near.

At the Tabularium, to which the third section of your ticket entitles you, too little is shown, and the apathy of the Roman official custodian is at its deepest. But in default of seeing the prisons you have placid views, remote from traffic, danger and noise, of the Forum. The dejected officials in uniform who sell the tickets and then sever them with the assistance of an obsolete bronze bar; the dejected men who then clip them and let you through a gate; the dejected men who desire the company of your walking-stick; and the dejected men who huddle rather than sit on chairs in the rooms, or cower over charcoal pans,—these are Rome's least happy citizens. Most Romans strike me as not discontented, even if not uproariously cheerful. But these custodians personify gloom in its depths. They brighten only when the opportunity arrives of saying that something you had set your heart upon seeing is "Chiuso."

The steps to the side of the Capitoline Museum lead to a pretty little loggia with three arches, in which are some almost obliterated frescoes. Turning to the left and ascending a little farther, you are in S. Maria in Aracœli, one of the pleasantest of Rome's churches, being set so high amid fresh air, and light and cheerful and full of interest. Every inch of it has colour, while the ceiling is richness indeed, a votive offering for the victory of Lepanto.

It was while meditating in this church that Gibbon decided to write his History of Rome's decline and fall—

THE CAPITOLINE HILL

"among the ruins of the Capitol" is the great historian's phrase—and the date was October 15, 1764. It was not until 1768, when he was thirty-one, that he really began his gigantic task, the preparations consisting of reading thousands and thousands of books. The first volume was published in 1776; in 1781 the second and third; and in 1788 the work was in the public's hands, complete. No one can rightly appreciate the older parts of Rome and especially the Forum, who has not read this work; and no one is to be more envied than the reader coming freshly to it.[1]

Rome cannot but sadden the sensitive observer, with its past of such grandeur and its sons so spendthrift of their treasure and careless of their heritage; and Gibbon, through digging so deeply into the records, was more conscious of the tragedy than any; more conscious also of the transitoriness of everything but dust. "The art of man," he wrote, "is able to construct monuments far more permanent than the narrow span of his own existence; yet these monuments, like himself, are perishable and frail; and, in the boundless annals of time, his life and his labours must equally be measured as a fleeting moment."

Always homely and intimate and doing its duty, at Christmas the church of S. Maria in Aracœli is gayest and busiest of all, because of the famous Bambino treasured there, which at that season is duly placed in a manger for the pious to visit and revere; while a separate, but allied attraction, is a recitation competition among the children of the parish. I once watched a little bunch of them gathered on a rostrum, each in turn delivering its piece with the same orotundity and the same gestures.

---

[1] Not only Gibbon, although the feast that he provides is the most splendid and piquant. Mann's or Pastor's *History of the Popes* will also make Rome clearer at every step.

Gesture is so natural in the Italian that these could not be described as forced, but I suspected the controlling hand of a priest or nun at rehearsals for some weeks before the event. Fond parents were to be seen among the audience, but although many listened, I cannot describe the attention as profound; while the other children waiting to take the platform were frankly conversational among themselves, often to the complete drowning of the tiny performer's voice. That recognition of naturalness and its rights which is one of the characteristics of the Church of Rome was never more noticeable. You would have thought that here, at any rate, and if at any time, some one in authority might have been present. But no, and no one minded. There was even a little knot of children playing with an air balloon at the outside edge of the audience.

Beginning at the right aisle, we find in the first chapel frescoes by the always delightful Pinturicchio, but they are faded. The colossal statue of Gregory XIII, with a very long neck, is one of a series of such figures, Paul III being opposite. In the left transept will be found Leo X, near the tomb of St. Helena. Standing before the high altar you should remember that Raphael's Madonna da Foligno (now in the Vatican picture gallery) was painted for it and for many years was honoured here. The present altar-piece is one of the Madonnas painted by St. Luke. The long flight of steps to the church came from the Temple of the Sun on the Quirinale. The brick façade looks as though it had been robbed of its marble, but there was never any. The circular windows are charming.

It might be as well to complete this visit by a glimpse of the Tarpeian Rock, from which criminals condemned to death were flung. You take the Via di Tor de' Specchi, just across the bottom of the Capitoline steps, and then

THE FORUM, LOOKING SOUTHEAST, SHOWING THE COLOSSEUM
AND CAMPANILE OF S. CLEMENTE IN THE FAR DISTANCE
AND THE COLUMNS OF THE TEMPLE OF CASTOR
IN THE FOREGROUND

[*See page* 174

the second turn to the left, which brings you to the foot of the fatal precipice. The Via di Tor de' Specchi is a very ancient and unsavoury street, every house in which is like a fortress, now cut into tenements; but it leads to worse, for we come out by the walls of the Theatre of Marcellus, which is the centre of the Ghetto. I do not counsel much wandering here, where godliness, we must hope, has taken the place of the other virtue.

Chapter XVII

The Forum and the Palatine

The Mamertine Prison—S. Adriano in Foro—The Twelve Pagan Gods—The Arch of Septimius Severus—The Forum and the Authorities—Guides—The House of Augustus—The House of Livia—The Villa Mills—The Circus Maximus—Julius Cæsar—Shakespeare.

MOST visitors, having looked down at the Forum from the Tabularium, or adjacent points of vantage on the Capitoline hill, descend and enter it; and, of course, to most visitors, the Forum is Rome's principal possession after St. Peter's, coming before either the Vatican or the Colosseum by moonlight. When I say the Forum, I mean the Forum Romanorum, the whole of that vast series of ruins of temples and public buildings between the Capitol and the Arch of Titus, to which are naturally added the remains of the Emperor's residences on the Palatine hill. Other cities have sublime and beautiful cathedrals; others have amphitheatres; but Rome alone has the Forum and the palaces of the Cæsars. Amid the stupendous relics of these abodes of magnificence one may walk for ever with an imagination almost painfully quickened.

Descending the Capitoline by the steps to the Arch of Septimius Severus, you skirt some very squalid quarters, their grime being intensified by their proximity to the dazzling new Vittorio Emmanuele II Memorial, which has poor relations indeed. The conspiracy to establish St. Peter in Rome—and, as I have said in other chapters, there is a possibility that he did come here—gains

170

strength at the Mamertine prison, a dreadful hole in the ground, without any air, to which the curious descend. The story is that both St. Peter and St. Paul were thrown here, and during captivity converted the guard and a number of other prisoners; while St. Peter, performing a miracle, produced from the rock water for his parched companions. The saints are said to have been there for several months, unwilling to escape because they did not think it right.

Above is a little chapel dedicated to St. Peter, and opposite is the church of SS. Martina e Luca, S. Martina, whose tomb may be visited in the crypt, being very cruelly martyred in the reign of Severus. Opposite S. Martina e Luca, is S. Adriano in Foro, the church whose blank brick wall, with a blind door in it, abuts on the Forum, and in one of whose niches you see a skeleton. Here once was Julius Cæsar's Curia, on the ruins of which this church was built, in honour of a Roman officer who was led to baptism through admiration of the courage of the martyrs whose death he had to witness. Subsequently he became a martyr himself. Ancient fluted pillars, enclosed in the square pillars of the church, are here and there visible. One of the most pleasing of the specially sacred Madonna altar-pieces of Rome is in a side chapel.

Before we enter the Forum there is much to be seen from the roadway between it and the Capitoline hill, and this is almost the only part of it where a book without a map can be helpful. In the Forum itself there is too much to see, and it is too congested for the written word to be sufficiently clear.

Beginning at the foot of the Via del Campidoglio and keeping to the Tabularium side of the road, the first row of pillars belong to the Porticus Deorum Consentium, an interesting and unexpected building, because this is all that remains of the colonnade on which twelve pagan gods were to be honoured, built in 367 by the Prefect Vettius Agorius Prætestatus in an attempt to restore the old faith which Constantine (306-337) had undermined. Julian the Apostate (360-363) had returned to paganism, and the temple of his Prefect was a legacy of that forlorn hope.

The next pillars, three in number, are those of the Temple of Vespasian, which his son Domitian (81-96) erected. The next, the Temple of Concordia, is much earlier in date—in fact 366 B.C.—and was rebuilt by Tiberius in 7 B.C.

On the Forum side of the road we find, immediately opposite the Temple of Concordia, and giving us one of the levels of the Forum at that day, the arch of Septimius Severus, set up in 203 in honour of the Emperor and his sons Caracalla and Geta and their victories over various foes. A bronze chariot with six horses once surmounted it. No doubt one of the entrances to the Forum would be through this arch; but the main road, the Via Sacra, was a few yards farther back, towards our starting-point at the Via del Campidoglio, running thence beside the Basilica Julia, and winding to the left and then on again to the Arch of Titus at the far end.

Still looking through the railings we see, close to the Arch of Septimius Severus, a small circular brick building. This was the Umbilicus Urbis, or navel of the city, from which all distances were measured; and about here, long buried, are vestiges of what are thought to be the earliest pagan temples. The temple of which eight columns survive is that of Saturn, known to have been consecrated as early as 497 B.C. The single column, near to us, is one of the youngest relics here, the column of Phocas, dating from 608, the last structure to be set up.

All this while we have been looking through the railings. To get to the entrance of the Forum we must go to the

THE FORUM AND THE PALATINE

left, at the end of the Via Cavour; to get to the entrance
of the Palatine, to the right, in the Via Teodoro; while at
the far end, by the Arch of Titus, there is another entrance
to both.

The Forum, although it has an increasing fascination
for me, never fails to make me deeply melancholy. First
because it is the tomb of so much splendour and power;
next because it is the memorial of so much folly; and
lastly because it is a testimony to so much deplorable
indifference in the past, when, beneath the eyes of Rome's
citizens and rulers, it was permitted to be both a quarry
for marble and a refuse dump.

I am pained, too, by the attitude of the authorities of
to-day, in their complete failure to recognize that they
owe any kind of paternal duty to the public who pay to
enter its gates.

Rome does very little for any one, anywhere, and almost
nothing for the sight-seer. It would be agreeable to
receive the appointment of editor of the city and at once
get to work to set up explanatory notices. They are
needed everywhere and, considering how important to
Rome are her character as a museum and the revenue
from abroad which that character brings to her, they
should everywhere be. But only a few exhibits in any
of the great sculpture galleries bear anything but a
number—useful to the purchaser of a catalogue (if there
is a catalogue) but useless to the poor; while in the Forum,
where every stone has not only its own history, but probably covers a deposit of earlier history, not one word of
information is provided, nor is there any official book of
assistance. Roman cynicism, self-satisfaction, detach-
ment—whatever you call it—nowhere is more evident.

The result is that for the Forum and the Palatine one
of the licensed guides is almost a necessity. That we
should be shown the Vatican sculpture and frescoes by a

guide is a distasteful thought: the ordinary kind of guide
has nothing to do with æsthetics; but he can throw welcome
light on ruins. Cultured lecturers are accessible through
most of the hotel bureaux, and these, of course, are best;
but for those who dislike joining parties and receiving
their impressions in massed formation, the guide who
hangs about the gates is a sufficient intermediary between
themselves and their history books, even though his English is broken and his knowledge fragmentary.

Here more than anywhere in Rome is Gibbon illumin-
ative. Without some memory of his music, his melancholy,
his irony and his contempt, no one can enjoy Rome to the
full, and particularly the palaces of the Cæsars, every
crumbling stone of which is a footnote to his work.

On every day, even in the rain, the Forum and the
Palatine are speckled by investigators, some alone, con-
sulting books or maps, some in couples (Love among the
Ruins), some in little parties being conducted. But on
Sundays the place is crowded. I like it best on that day;
I like to watch the reaction of these past glories on the less
sophisticated visitors from poorer Rome and the
Campagna.

The guide will show you all the regular things; and
while he is talking you will see others for yourself—such
as the griffins in relief over the portico of the temple of
Antoninus and Faustina, which is now S. Lorenzo, and
the coloured marbles in the floors of the Basilica Emilia,
and the roses beside the pools in the atrium of the House
of the Vestals. When you are looking at the Basilica
Julia, remember (or so I have been told) that the vast
church of St. Paul's-outside-the-walls (S. Paolo fuori le
Mura) reproduces its dimensions and its pillars, and this
will enable you to get an idea of it before all those groves
of columns were felled.

It is odd that while there is a lift to the Pincio from

the Piazza di Spagna, there should be none from the low
level of the Forum to the Farnese Cascino. Many a
visitor to Rome who walks not too strongly must have
been denied the amazing adventure of the Palatine altogether; because there is no roadway for vehicles, no lift
and none of Pompeii's litters. Since Rome profits hugely
by the entrance fees to its public show-places, something
more, you would think, might be done. It is true that the
Forum and the Palatine may be seen free on Sunday; but,
for some reason, not the House of Livia.

Livia, who gives her name to this charming little abode,
which, whatever else is scamped among these overwhelm-
ing ruins, must be seen, was the wife of Augustus and
the mother of Tiberius. What remains of it conveys perhaps the best idea of the good taste of these Roman homes,
so much mural decoration being left. I doubt if anything
is quite so fine as the Aldobrandini Nuptials which we saw
in the Vatican Library, but the whole place, if less gay,
is more distinguished than the Casa dei Vettii at Pompeii.
Note the completeness of the heating system.

The forlorn abandoned château, or palace, or casino,
on the highest part of the hill with its mixed architecture
and commanding loggias, was once the Villa Mills, the
Roman residence of a wealthy Englishman. Before that
it had belonged to a Roman family, and dates from the
seventeenth century. After the Mills era it was a nunnery. Now it is yet another—but compared with the
Cæsars' palaces how flimsy!—monument to Decay. It is
from the edges of its garden that you get certain fine
prospects of Rome and that amazing downward view of
the stadium of Augustus; but it is from the Belvedere on
the other side of the stadium that a famous panorama of
Rome is gained.

From this point the outlines of the gigantic Circus
Maximus, immediately below, may be traced: an arena in

the valley between the two hills. The circus could hold two hundred thousand people—some authorities say between three and four hundred thousand—at a time when Rome's population was two millions. It was from this Circus Maximus that the obelisk in the centre of the Piazza del Popolo and the obelisk at the Lateran were taken. A promise has been made by Signor Mussolini that it shall be excavated and to some extent restored, and this great task should yield very valuable results. It was last used as a place of entertainment in 510, when a naval battle was re-enacted there.

It is no part of the scheme of this rambling impressionistic book to narrate with any order the early history of Rome. I take it for granted that the reader is aware that before the Cæsars Rome was a republic administered by consuls and prefects; that with the advent of Julius Cæsar came its new and more splendid era as an empire; that its religion was the worship of many departmental gods under one godhead, Jupiter.

In the Forum itself there is no need for history earlier than the time of Julius Cæsar, even though many of the buildings of his reign were superimposed upon others more ancient. It is with him that Rome may at the moment be said to begin. If very little of the Forum which we now see could have met his eye, it was still he who planned the new Rome, even though his great successor, Augustus, completed many of his projects. Hence it is with these that we are concerned, leaving the great builders under the Republic to be sought for in the history books.

Apropos of Julius Cæsar, it is well before entering the Forum to purge one's mind of all memory of elaborate representations of Shakespeare's Roman plays. The difference between the stage producer's idea of the platform on which Marc Antony delivered his oration over Julius

MARCUS AURELIUS AS A YOUTH
After the Bust in the Capitoline Museum

[*See page* 163

THE WOLF WITH ROMULUS AND REMUS
After the Statue in the Capitoline Museum

[*See page* 164

Photographs by Anderson

THE WOLF WITH ROMULUS AND REMUS
Detail of the Picture by RUBENS *in the Capitoline Museum*

[*See page* 165

THE FORUM AND THE PALATINE

Cæsar's body and the actual structure as it has been preserved is immense. Shakespeare, with his great gentleman's genius, made everything as it ought to have been. There is no harm, when in the Colosseum, or when looking down from the Palatine heights over the site of the Circus Maximus, in remembering Gérome's grandiose pictures "Pollice Verso" and "Christiani ad Leones"; their authority cannot be undermined; but recollections of the stage are fatal.

Another disappointment is the lake, which the guide will indicate, into which Metius Curtius plunged on horseback to save the city from the anger of the gods.

In looking at the Forum, now such a mass of ruins and the ruins of ruins, of different periods of antiquity, as to be, in the aggregate, without meaning, or, except under favourable conditions of weather, any beauty save that of disorder, it is well to remember that this once was, in little, what all Rome is to-day: that is to say, there were busy streets here, still traceable, lined with shops and offices; there were large market-halls; there were temples (in place of churches); there were large government buildings; and there were platforms for oratory. The Forum was, in fact, the natural place for buying and selling, for conversation, and for public gatherings. One of the structures least difficult to re-erect in the mind's eye is the rostrum. With the Capitoline bust of Cicero to assist you, you may even believe yourself listening to that orator.

CHAPTER XVIII

The Forum and the Emperors

Julius Cæsar—*Lays of Ancient Rome*—The Emperor Augustus—
Perished Fora—Tiberius—Caligula—Nero—Vespasian—Titus and
Domitian—Nerva—Trajan's Forum—A Cat's Home—Hadrian—
Antoninus Pius—Marcus Aurelius and his Faith—A Roman Emperor
in England—Diocletian—Constantine the Great—The Galilean's
Conquest.

GAIUS JULIUS CÆSAR, who was born of patrician
stock in the year 102 B.C., claimed to be of the
divine line through Iulus, son of Æneas and grandson
of Venus. Cæsar's temple to his ancestress in his own
Forum has vanished, but his tribune in the Forum Romanorum is shown, from which Marc Antony delivered
his oration and near which the body of the murdered
ruler was burned. His Basilica Julia, begun in 46 and
finished by Augustus, is now nothing but a magnificent
ghost. His Curia Julia, or house of the Senate, was transformed into a Christian church in the seventh century,
when the fashion for reclaiming pagan structures set
in, and is now S. Adriano. As to his own places of worship—of the temple of Jupiter on the Capitol there is now
no trace; while the temple of Juno, adjoining it, is now
lost beneath S. Maria in Aracœli. In both of those
buildings Cæsar would have made oblations; and he would
also have bowed the knee in the temple of Castor and
Pollux in the Forum, set high on its mound, of which the
three splendid columns remain—three columns which are,
through reproductions due to the activity of the sculp-

tors and modellers, almost as much a symbol of Rome
as the dome of St. Peter's itself.

The temple of Castor and Pollux, which would have
been familiar to Julius Cæsar all his life, was erected in
honour of the victory of the Romans over the Latins at
the battle of Lake Regillus in 496 B.C—the battle celebrated by Macaulay in one of the *Lays of Ancient Rome*.
As for that better known Lay, describing how Horatius
kept the bridge, history seems to know little, nor have I
found any one to tell me where the bridge was situated.
Anyway, it is one of the great ballads, and I must not be
denied the pleasure of quoting its beautiful concluding
stanzas here, while Ancient Rome is our theme:—

> . . . They made a molten image,
>   And set it up on high,
> And there it stands unto this day
>   To witness if I lie.
>
> It stands in the Comitium,
>   Plain for all folk to see;
> Horatius in his harness,
>   Halting upon one knee:
> And underneath is written,
>   In letters all of gold,
> How valiantly he kept the bridge
>   In the brave days of old.
>
> And still his name sounds stirring
>   Unto the men of Rome,
> As the trumpet-blast that cries to them
>   To charge the Volscian home;
> And wives still pray to Juno
>   For boys with hearts as bold
> As his who kept the bridge so well
>   In the brave days of old.

A WANDERER IN ROME

And in the nights of winter,
  When the cold north winds blow,
And the long howling of the wolves
  Is heard amidst the snow;
When round the lonely cottage
  Roars loud the tempest's din,
And the good logs of Algidus
  Roar louder yet within;

When the oldest cask is opened,
  And the largest lamp is lit;
When the chestnuts glow in the embers,
  And the kid turns on the spit;
When young and old in circle
  Around the firebrands close;
When the girls are weaving baskets,
  And the lads are shaping bows.

When the goodman mends his armour,
  And trims his helmet's plume;
When the goodwife's shuttle merrily
  Goes flashing through the loom;
With weeping and with laughter
  Still is the story told,
How well Horatius kept the bridge
  In the brave days of old.

Julius Cæsar's own Forum, not to be confounded with
the Forum Romanorum, covered the district between S.
Adriano, the Via Bonella, the Via della Marmorelle and
the Via Cremona. The temple which he raised to Venus
Genetrix was beside the Via Cremona, where shops now
are.

This great man with the beautiful head, under whom
Britain became a Roman colony, and Rome was shaped
into a civilization from which the world still borrows, was
murdered in 44 B.C. His successor was his nephew,

THE FORUM AND THE EMPERORS

Gaius Julius Cæsar Octavianus, who in that year was twenty-one. At first he had to be content with only a share of power, divided between himself and such rivals as Brutus, Cassius, Sextus Pompeius and Marc Antony. The defeat of Marc Antony and Cleopatra, and their suicide in 31, put Octavian into complete authority, and in 27 B.C. the Senate conferred upon him the honour of the name Augustus, meaning venerable and majestic; and as Augustus he is known, and Augustan his golden age. The name meant more than that: it meant Emperor. Julius Cæsar had been only "Dictator"; Augustus was the first Emperor.

There was much war during his reign, but there was time also to cultivate the arts and to do much towards beautifying the Forum. There also was enough peace to justify the erection of the Ara Pacis, the sublime monument fragments of which may be seen here and there. In the chapter on the Corso I have said where its gate was. Augustus was the friend of Horace and Virgil and the close associate of their patron, Mæcenas, and when the Emperor restored to Rome the secular games Horace wrote the processional hymn, the *Carmen Seculare*. We have seen on the Palatine the remains of the palace of Augustus and the house of his beloved wife Livia, whom he had married in 38. Even from the ruins we get an impression of bland and thoughtful culture.

Augustus not only did much to complete Cæsar's Forum Romanorum, but he built a Forum of his own, traces of which remain in the district where we now find the Via Bonella and the Via Alessandrina. The triumphal arch of Augustus in the Forum Romanorum, in the Via Sacra, near the house of the Vestal Virgins and between the temple of Castor and Pollux and Cæsar's pyre, was erected in honour of the defeat of the Parthians. Three Corinthian columns of the temple of Mars, built by Augustus and dedicated in 2 B.C., remain in the Via Bonella, where are visible other traces of its splendour. It was in the reign of Augustus that Christ was born, and in the reign of Tiberius, his successor, that Christ was crucified.

Tiberius, in fact, during the last years of the life of Augustus, assisted him in administration. This ruler (the son of Livia by her first husband), who had proved himself an admirable general in many campaigns, did not long continue on the best road but grievously lowered the standard of personal conduct set by Augustus. The triumphal arch of Tiberius, at the beginning of the Via Sacra, was built by him in A.D. 16 in honour of the victories over the Germanic tribes by his brother Drusus, who might, had he lived, have been a greater than himself. In honour of his stepfather and predecessor Tiberius built the temple of Augustus (who, like Julius Cæsar, had been placed by the Romans among the gods), traces of which remain beside the Vicus Tuscus, the ancient street under the Palatine hill adjoining the place of Caligula. Here we now find the remains of the frescoed church of S. Maria Antiqua, a sixth-century building, in which the library of the temple of Augustus is embodied. Tiberius also had his palace on the Palatine, but nothing of it remains. The present maze in the Farnese gardens would seem to be above the very centre of it.

To Tiberius succeeded Caligula, the madman, much brickwork of whose palace on the Palatine may be seen, but nothing is left of his great Circus on the site of which much of St. Peter's and the Piazza of St. Peter's stands.

Caligula was succeeded by Claudius, grandson of Livia and nephew of Tiberius, and he too leaves little trace. This emperor, a criminally weak creature, was handicapped by his marriage with the notorious Messalina, and afterwards with Agrippina, Caligula's sister, whose ambition for her son Nero led her to Claudius's murder. It was under Claudius that the fine aqueduct, some of the arches of which we see from the Via S. Gregorio crossing to the Palatine, was built—the Aqua Claudia. The Porta Maggiore, where the curious tomb of Eurysaces, the baker, is seen, was once merely an archway of this aqueduct.

We now reach the dreaded name of Nero, who succeeded in 54 and built, destroyed and rebuilt. Nero, who came to the throne when he was only a youth, behaved at first with modesty and circumspection; but his true colours soon showed themselves. His chief obstacles to absolutism, his mother and Britannicus, being removed by murder, and his wife, of whom he had wearied, by divorce, he gave himself to indulgence, not discouraged by his new wife Poppæa. This is no place for account of his enormities and the savage delight that he took in the persecution of the new sect called Christians. The burning of Rome, which he is said himself to have started as a spectacle, fiddling the while, was a culmination; but history has few facts. His rebuilding centred chiefly in his own Golden House on the Esquiline hill, which is gradually being excavated, the entrance being in the Via Labicana. This palace was probably the most sumptuous and extravagant abode ever decreed, covering, with its lawns and woods and lakes, the ground between the Palatine and the Esquiline where the Colosseum now stands and far up the hill. Of the disasters of Nero's reign, which included very serious revolt in Britain, and of his insane personal vanities, I have no room to speak. He died at the early age of thirty-one and with him the blood line of Cæsars came to an end. During the persecutions of his reign St. Paul was put to death.

It is possible that St. Peter was also martyred then; but it may have been under Galba, the new emperor, who was practically self-appointed and made no mark during

his year's reign. He was killed in the Forum, near the
Lacus Curtius, in 69, and was succeeded by his vanquisher
Otho, to whom followed Vitellius. It was in the reign
of Galba that the first Pope was elected—Linus (67-76.)

The next great name is that of Vespasian (69-79) the
son of a tax-collector. A capable soldier, he was for a
while in command of the Roman forces in Britain, and
later it was he who despatched Agricola to that island
to colonize it. As a ruler Vespasian was wise and thor-
ough and Rome prospered under him. His own Forum
covered the ground at the back of the church of SS.
Cosma e Damiano, where the Via Alessandrina and the
Via Miranda now run, and it was he who began the
Colosseum. He was the patron of Pliny and is credited
with the famous remark, "An Emperor should die standing." We saw, while still outside the Forum, under the
Tabularium, some columns of the temple of Vespasian,
erected by his son, Domitian.

Both of Vespasian's sons, Titus and Domitian, became
emperors. Titus (79-81), who had shared authority with
his father for some years, is the author of the saying
"Perdidi diem," uttered at the close of every day on which
he had made no one happy with a gift. It was during his
reign that Pompeii and Herculaneum were destroyed. The
Arch of Titus was erected in honour of his conquest of
the Jews. He finished the Colosseum begun by his father,
and gave Rome some magnificent baths, which have now
been built over.

Titus died naturally, but his brother Domitian (81-
96), who was publicly a stern censor of morals, but pri-
vately a very decadent character and a bitter foe to the
Christians, was assassinated. One of Domitian's acts
was to restore the Temple of Jupiter on the Capitol,
which had been burned down in the reign of his father

S. LORENZO IN MIRANDA, BUILT BEHIND THE COLUMNS
OF THE TEMPLE OF ANTONINUS AND FAUSTINA.
THE TORRE DELLE MILIZIE, OR NERONE, IN THE DISTANCE

[*See page* 187

THE FORUM AND THE EMPERORS

Vespasian. It remained the pagan cathedral of Rome until Christianity sounded its doom.

Domitian was succeeded by Nerva (96-98) whose Forum, begun by Domitian, was between those of Vespasian and Augustus, where the Via della Croce Bianca now runs. It included a temple to Minerva, and when you are on the Janiculum hill looking at that glorious gushing fountain, the Aqua Paolina, remember that it was from this temple that its marble was taken. Nerva was not a soldier, but a lawyer, and his equable good sense was a value after the disquiet under the treacherous Domitian, the last few years of whose life were complicated by insanity.

Nerva himself selected Trajan as his successor and for a while allowed him to rule; and the choice could not have been better, for that Emperor, who rose from the ranks to the highest honour the world then held, restored Rome to health. Not only did he himself live plainly, but he endeavoured to get his people to do the same. The public demand for "panem et circenses" (bread and entertainments) never was so punctually fulfilled as under him, while he was universally respected and even beloved, not only for this concession, but for his reasonableness in taxation. As a military genius his fame is kept alive by the famous column in his Forum, the Trajan column, where in a winding scroll of reliefs may be seen the record of his victory over the Dacians. The figure of the Emperor on the top was, however, taken down by Pope Sixtus V and that of St. Peter substituted—an unwarrantable act. In order to make this Forum, Trajan excavated an enormous amount of earth from the Quirinal and Capitoline hills, and indeed formed an artificial valley. How much was dug can be computed from the fact that the top of the column is the old level of the ground. The column is just under 100 feet in height; and there is a spiral staircase inside, but I have never ascended it.

Trajan's Forum has one peculiarity that is never lacking: at whatever time you peer over the edge into the abyss of broken pedestals and all the débris of fallen splendour, you will see half a dozen lean and predatory cats. The four rows of columns in the Forum were those of the Basilica Ulpia, a vast temple, as large as S. Paolo fuori le Mura, which stood here in Trajan's time. The restaurant Ulpia now occupies a portion of it, and you eat among the ruins of the pagan faith.

Among Trajan's other gifts to Rome was the aqueduct that brought water to Rome from Lake Bracciano, modernized under Pope Paul V. Trajan's baths were above Titus's on the Esquiline hill, where the Via delle Sette Sale now runs.

After Trajan came his adopted son Hadrian (117-138) of whom I say something in the chapter on his tomb, now known as the Castel Sant' Angelo. One of the most dramatic moments in the history of Trajan's Forum must have been the burning in public of the taxation bonds, when Hadrian came to the throne, by which act the people of Rome were released from a debt of about ten million pounds sterling; and you should be sure to ask the guide in the Forum Romanorum to lead the way to the Anaglypha Trajani, the two marble balustrades decorated on one side with animals and on the other with reliefs, because not only are they beautiful, but they illustrate the burning of the bonds and other events of that time and include contemporary representations of certain of the Forum buildings.

The next great name is that of Hadrian's successor Antoninus Pius (138-161) whom Hadrian adopted as his son and who earned his sobriquet by inducing the Roman people to grant his adopted father divine honours. He was a kindly benevolent man and a friend to learning and to light. The church of S. Lorenzo on the edge of the Forum was built on the foundations of the temple of Antoninus and his wife Faustina, preserving the colonnade and the beautiful reliefs. Just as Hadrian had adopted Antoninus, so had Antoninus adopted Marcus Aurelius, his wife's nephew, as well as Lucius Ælius Verus. Both became Emperors.

Of Marcus Aurelius Antoninus (161-180) I have said something in the chapter in which his Column is mentioned. Here it may be added that his *Meditations* is still a work which, although he was a determined foe to the new religion, Christians may read with profit. His opposition to Christians did not amount to persecution; he merely, as the head of the religion of Rome, discountenanced and discouraged any non-conformity to its rules and practices.

Let me quote a passage or so from the Emperor's account of his early education. "From my grandfather Verus," he begins, "I learned good morals and the government of my temper.

"From the reputation and remembrance of my father, modesty and a manly character.

"From my mother, piety and beneficence, and abstinence, not only from evil deeds, but even from evil thoughts; and further, simplicity in my way of living, far removed from the habits of the rich.

"From Fronto I learned to observe what envy, and duplicity, and hypocrisy are in a tyrant, and that generally those among us who are called Patricians are rather deficient in paternal affection.

"From Alexander the Platonic, not frequently nor without necessity to say to any one, or to write in a letter, that I have no leisure; nor continually to excuse the neg-

lect of duties required by our relation to those with whom
we live by alleging urgent occupations.

"From Maximus I learned self-government and not to
be led aside by anything; and cheerfulness in all circum-
stances, as well as in illness; and a just admixture in the
moral character of sweetness and dignity, and to do what
was set before me without complaining. . . . I observed
that no man could ever think that he was despised by
Maximus, or ever venture to think himself a better man.
He had also the art of being humorous in an agreeable
way.

"To the gods I am indebted for having good grand-
fathers, good parents, a good sister, good teachers, good
associates, good kinsmen and friends, nearly everything
good. Further, I owe it to the gods that I was not
hurried into any offence against any of them, though I
had a disposition which, if opportunity had offered, might
have led me to do something of this kind; but through
their favour there never was such a concurrence of circum-
stances as put me to the trial.

"I thank the gods for giving me such a brother, who
was able by his moral character to rouse me to vigilance
over myself, and who, at the same time, pleased me by
his respect and affection; that my children have not been
stupid nor deformed in body; that I did not make more
proficiency in rhetoric, poetry and other studies, in which
I should perhaps have been completely engaged, if I had
seen that I was making progress in them."

Finally, he thanks the gods that "though it was my
mother's fate to die young, she spent the last years of her
life with me; that, whenever I wished to help any man in
need, or on any other occasion, I was never told that I
had not the means of doing it; and that to myself the
same necessity never happened to receive anything from
another; that I have such a wife, so obedient, and so

THE FORUM AND THE EMPERORS

affectionate, and so simple; that I had abundance of
good masters for my children . . . and that when I had
an inclination to philosophy, I did not fall into the hands
of any sophist, and that I did not waste my time on
writers of histories or in the resolution of syllogisms, or
occupy myself about the investigation of appearances in
the heavens."

The pious Antoninus' other adopted son, Lucius Ælius
Verus, who succeeded Marcus Aurelius as Commodus and
reigned from 180 to 192, was a very different character.
He displayed cruel and tyrannical tendencies, spent much
time in gladiatorial contests in public, and was eventually
murdered.

Passing over the names of Pertinax and Didius Juli-
anus, we come to Septimius Severus (193-212) to whom
the Arch of Severus, under the Tabularium, was erected,
and who was succeeded by his depraved son Caracalla
(212-217), the builder of the great baths which we shall
see on the way to the Porta S. Sebastiano. Severus, I
might remark, spent the last three years of his life in endeavouring to allay trouble in Britain, and he died at
York, which was then known as Eboracum; the only Roman Emperor to meet his end on our soil. His Roman
palace was on the Palatine, on the far side beyond the
deep and massive stadium of Augustus. The Belvedere,
from which the view over the Circus Maximus is obtained,
is built on its ruins.

We may now skip fifty years, during which emperors
of less importance reigned, and come to Aurelian (270-
275) who rose from the ranks to the throne and was a
great soldier. He worked hard for the well-being of
Rome at home too, and the wall which still encircles the
city was of his devising. His assassination by his secre-
tary was a grievous blow.

Again skipping, we come to Diocletian (284-305) whose

189

name was made poignantly memorable by his martyrdom
of the Christians. He too was of the people and rose
through arms. As a domestic administrator he was capable and shrewd, and even his filling of the catacombs
has been defended on the grounds of the necessity of unity
of control in a State, the new sect having developed into
what he thought was tantamount to a secret society.
Among his buildings are the baths that bear his name,
near the station, in the midst of which Michael Angelo,
twelve centuries later, built the church and monastery of
S. Maria degli Angeli, the cloisters of which are now the
Museo Nazionale.

After a negligible year or so we come to one of the
greatest names of all—Constantine the Great (306-337),
who for a while had only a divided empire, but consoli-
dated it in 324. Of Constantine and his mother St.
Helena I speak in the chapter on the Lateran. His kindness to Christianity and final acceptance of its tenets were
not sufficient to make it lawful, but under his successors it
was tolerated, if not blessed. The arch erected in his
honour, near the Colosseum, with the husk of a fountain
beside it—the oldest of all Rome's many fountains, but no
longer playing—was erected in honour of his final defeat
of his imperial rival Maxentius, in the battle in which Constantine was assisted by celestial allies—as represented
in Raphael's cartoon in the Vatican. In order to make
this arch, earlier buildings were levied upon, in the sacri-
legious Roman way. Hence the presence of Trajan on
certain of the reliefs. The fountain, the Meta Sudans,
was constructed by Domitian.

Constantine had no Forum of his own, but to the Forum
Romanorum he added the vast basilica, the commanding
shell of which still stands, while one of its eight columns
may be seen opposite S. Maria Maggiore, giving an idea
of its size and magnificence. Bramante adopted the meas-

urement of the vaulting of these great arches for the nave of St. Peter's.

Constantine was the last of the Emperors to leave any mark on the Forum. His nephew Julian, born in Constantinople, a man of ideals and culture rather than of action, did little for Rome and was little there. His devotion to the old gods did not make him a persecutor of the Christians; he merely distrusted them and sought to limit their power, just as the Jews have been mistrusted everywhere, and as in England until quite recent times the Roman Catholics were not allowed to hold office.

Julian's dying words, in 363, are said to have been "Thou hast conquered, O Galilean,"—referring probably to the actual cause of death, a sword-thrust from a Christian soldier—but they were true in the larger sense too. There was no stemming this tide, and soon after Theodosius came to the throne in 379 Christianity had its chance. Theodosius was of Christian parentage, but it was not until in the fear of death that he was baptized. That was in 380, and immediately afterwards he issued a decree making the faith of St. Peter and Pope Damasus, exemplified in the Nicene Creed, the true faith, with punishment in store for those who did not subscribe to it. Thus, although disputes and factional divisions were to follow, was Christianity established.

Theodosius is the last Emperor to mention, although a word might be said of his poor son Honorius (395-423) who added to Aurelian's Wall and under whom Britain was lost to Rome.

Chapter XIX

The Colosseum and Some Churches

The Roman Builders—Nero's End—A Home of Gigantic Spectacle—The Decline of the Colosseum—Guides again—A Modern Circus—The Roman Audience—SS. Cosmas and Damianus—The Temple of Romulus—A Door in the Air—S. Francesca Romana—The Fall of Simon Magus—Two Hillside Churches—Pope Gregory the Great—The Conversion of England—A House beneath a Church—SS. Quattro Coronati—The Martyrs' Picture Gallery—S. Clemente—Sacrificial Rites.

O N leaving the Forum by the far end we have before us the great bulk of the Colosseum, with its massive blocks of stone and its rows of beautiful grave arches. The accuracy and activity of very ancient builders are always a matter for admiration and wonder; but to my mind the bricklayer of Rome in the great days is even more remarkable than the stonemason. Solid and immense as are Rome's palaces of rock and marble, intricate as are her domes and colonnades, it is when one stands among the ruins on the far side of the Palatine, where the Cæsars set slaves to work, that you best realize the stupendous structural energy of these people. Not even the Colosseum blocks posed truly one on the other without mortar, impress me more than these gigantic walls of brick.

The low site of the Colosseum is due to the circumstance that it occupies the site which Nero, whose palace, or Golden House covered the neighbouring slopes of the Esquiline, hollowed out and converted into a lake. After Nero's death in A.D. 68 (but the legend in Rome was that

192

S. BRUNO

After the Statue by HOUDON *in the*
Church of S. Maria degli Angeli

[*See page* 213

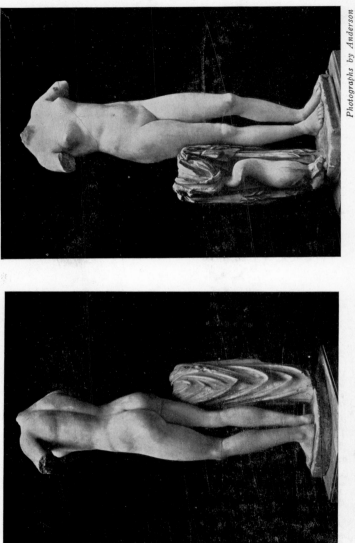

THE VENUS OF CYRENE
After the Statue in the Museo Nazionale

[*See page* 214

he was not dead but lived monstrously on in dark hiding)
his house was neglected, and when Vespasian, who came
to the throne in 69, began the Colosseum, it was from this
ill-fated palace that he took the marble. It was then to
be called Vespasian's Circus. The proximity of the colossal statue of Nero, later to be erected by Hadrian, gave
it its present name.

When Vespasian died in 79, the building was incomplete,
and Titus, his son and successor, finished it. The opening
performances lasted for one hundred days, the spectacles
comprising naval manœuvres and the slaying of five thousand wild beasts. The flooding apparatus is easily reconstructed in the mind's eye; indeed enough evidence remains to prove that there is nothing of realism in present
day representations that the Roman producers did not
know. Another remarkable series of performances were
given in the year 248, under the Emperor Philip the
Arabian (244-249) to celebrate the thousandth anniversary of the founding of Rome. The last of these
great spectacles seems to have been held in 523, when the
Roman Empire existed no more. Since then various
calamities, chiefly earthquakes, damaged the Colosseum
from time to time, while its stores of marble were (in
their turn) steadily depleted to aggrandize other buildings. The Vatican took pity on it under Benedict XIV
(1740-1758) who dedicated it to the Passion of Christ.
The piers and buttresses that now make it secure as a ruin
were the work of Pius IX.

As in the Forum, it is wise here, and often amusing, to
let yourself be wax in the hands of a guide. He may be
wrong, but he will have enough that is right to make
everything a little more vivid. He also will tell you
about the necessary moonlight visit. Be sure, if you are
vigorous enough, to ascend to the highest galleries, from

which an idea of the "full house" may be gained as well as views of Rome.

Having spent the morning of a winter Sunday in the Colosseum endeavouring, in the mind's eye, thus to re-people its myriad seats while a Triumph was in progress —to see the sailors spreading the awning—to hear the Roman holiday-makers chattering and laughing—and to guess at the feelings of this vast concourse (so vast that when there was a good programme you would suppose the rest of Rome to be empty) as the bars were drawn and the wild beasts advanced upon the terrified groups of the baptized; having engaged in this excursion of imagination in an extinct circus, I visited later an active one, not a little on account of the big print of the posters promising "60 leoni." The opportunity of comparing the shadowy lions of my dream with sixty genuine specimens seemed too favourable, even though the Christians remained secure among the audience.

But alas! even in Rome the advertiser can delude. Domitian may be dead, but Mr. Crummles survives; and the lions had their being only on the placards. Still, it was an attractive show, with a fire-eater to provide a lesser thrill, and not the least entertaining thing about it was the sight of all the good Roman fathers carrying and nursing their children. For it was Sunday afternoon, and no one had left the children at home. They were everywhere, and always the fathers were being motherly.

Nothing, by the way, could be more different than the demeanour of the Romans in the circus and the Romans in the music-hall. In the circus they are pleased with everything, or, at any rate, nothing annoys them. They come with a cheerful expression ready for whatever is spread, and if they approve they applaud. But to the Salone Margherita, or any of the other music-halls, they

go apparently hoping only to be affronted, and their attitude is one of apathy, disdain, or censure. The singers
do their best, while the Romans read their papers—and
they are great paper-readers—at the end of each song
looking up just long enough to hiss.

The Colosseum may be taken as the centre of a circle
in which a number of interesting minor churches are to
be found beginning with those on the edge of the Forum
itself. I have spoken of S. Lorenzo superimposed on
the walls of the temple of Antoninus and Faustina; but
there is its neighbour still to see—SS. Cosmas and Damianus, the entrance to which is in the Via Miranda.

This is a cheerful church because it is always full of
ragamuffins from the adjoining school. Also it has delightful sixth-century mosaics in the tribune, where the
Twelve Apostles are represented by the artist as so
many sheep, with Christ, as the Lamb of God, in the midst.
The circular part of the church, where the school children sometimes enact little plays, was once the upper
part of the Temple of Romulus. If you can find the
sacristan, you should get him to take you down to the
church below, to the circular part, the lower portion of
the temple which abuts on to the Forum with its fine
bronze doors and two porphyry columns. Here in an
altar of translucent alabaster are the remains of the two
saints, Arabian physicians who became Christians and
were put to death by Diocletian. After being canonized
they became the patron saints of druggists, doctors,
barbers and dentists.

Reverting for a moment to S. Lorenzo—latterly it has
been closed as a church and any one in authority is difficult to find, but if you can get access you should, because
the door opposite the altar opens directly on to midair,
overlooking the Forum, high up, with no steps, and the

view from this spot, facing the Palatine, is very fine. Also you are an object of envy to every one down below.

The church at the Colosseum end of the Forum, between the basilica of Constantine and the Arch of Titus, with the thirteenth-century campanile of brick set with coloured medallions, is S. Francesca Romana, once S. Maria Nuova, and it is remarkable for containing yet another painting of the Madonna from the hand of St. Luke. The marble saint in the Confessio is S. Francesca de' Ponziani, or St. Frances of Rome, who founded an Order of Oblate nuns of Tor de' Spettri, died in 1440, and was canonized in 1608. She was adored by the poor of Rome for her piety and benefactions, not the less since for thirty years, it is said, she was accompanied by the visible presence of her guardian angel.

The stone on which St. Peter knelt when praying for the punishment of Simon Magus, is built into the walls on the right of the apse, and you are shown the actual imprint of the Saint's knees: a further testimony to the statement that the founder of the Papacy actually did inhabit this city.

Simon the Magician, I should say, had offered to reproduce, for Nero's entertainment, the miracle of the Ascension of Christ, and so to bring the new religion into ridicule. This would be about A.D. 54. All Rome assembled in the neighbouring Forum to see the experiment, including St. Peter. At the first essay the magician did actually rise in the air, whereupon St. Peter sank in supplication on the Via Sacra imploring Heaven that the trick should fail—with the result that Simon fell to earth, and, fallen, spattered the Emperor with his blood. A church of St. Peter stood on the site of this church, before it was called S. Maria Nuova and, naturally, after it had ceased to be a temple of Venus.

Beside the entrance to the Palatine, on the other side

of the Arch of Titus, is a steep winding footpath, the Vicolo di San Bonaventura, which leads to a series of Stations of the Cross and at the top to a little church in which is kept, under the altar, revealed and illumined for the devout by an attendant Franciscan monk, the preserved body, or the waxen image, of St. Leonard of Port-Maurice, placed as in death. St. Leonard, who died in the neighbouring monastery in 1751, was the founder of the first confraternity in Rome of the Sacred Heart. The bodies of St. Flavian and St. Columba, both martyrs, also are kept in this little church.

Halfway up the hill is the gate leading to the even smaller church of S. Sebastiano alla Polveriera, indicating that there was once a powder magazine here. In the apse are some faint frescoes, copies and reconstructions of which are displayed by the sacristan. St. Sebastian may well be honoured here, for he was a soldier before he was a saint (although very noticeably in the days before powder). There is a little waste garden adjoining the church in which you should stray for the view of the Colosseum.

If we leave the Colosseum by the Via S. Gregorio, we come to the church which gives its name to the street, standing on the hillside more or less on the site of the house of St. Gregory's father, Gordianus, a wealthy and important Roman citizen. St. Gregory, or Pope Gregory the Great, whose monument we saw in St. Peter's, was born here somewhere about the year 540, his mother Sylvia afterwards being also raised to the company of saints.

Pope Gregory's church is now in a poor way, mildewed and forlorn. I tried in vain to find some one to show me the little chapels in the garden, in one of which the Pope's mother should be reverenced, while in another is a statue of himself in which Michael Angelo may have had a hand.

A WANDERER IN ROME

So great a pontiff's own shrine might be better cared for.
You may sit in his marble armchair, placed in what pur-
ports to be his cell, and think of his interest in English
souls. It was from the Benedictine monastery on this
spot that first Gregory, and afterwards St. Augustine,
set forth, bent on bringing us peace and goodwill.

A little way down the Via S. Gregorio, also high on the
left, on this, the Celian, hill, you see the brick apse of a
church among monastic buildings, with delicate archways
in marble, gained by a steep and ancient path. We ought
to look at this church, for it is SS. Giovanni e Paolo and
there is more than at first meets the eye; surprisingly
more. St. John and St. Paul were not the apostles, but
two brothers, Roman officers, who suffered martyrdom in
the year 362, under Julian. A marble slab in the church
pavement marks the spot beneath which the execution
occurred, the church having been built over their house.

I have said elsewhere in this book that in Rome everything that you now see covers something else, and this is
peculiarly the case at the church of SS. Giovanni e Paolo,
for beneath its floor is a complete ancient Roman dwelling. We go normally to Pompeii for such relics, but this
house is in better repair than almost anything there.
When the church was built in the fourth century, it was
deliberately set over these rooms, which were filled with
earth for solidity. You would expect earth to be less
preservative than volcanic dust—even detrimental—but
no; when in 1887 the soil was removed and underpinning
substituted, the frescoes on the walls were undamaged.
Some are pagan, some Christian; you see the various
living rooms, even the wine and oil cellar.

The portico of the church was added by the English
Pope, Nicholas Breakspeare, of St. Albans, who took the
title Adrian IV (1154-1159)—the only Pope chosen from
our country, although others may have nearly been

elected, Cardinal Pole, for example, and possibly Wolsey. The very pretty campanile was added in 1206. In the grounds of the monastery are the remains of the Vivarium in which the lions and other wild animals required for the Colosseum performances were kept. Across the road from the church is an old garden now used by a film producing company!

While on the Celian heights we might look at two other churches, both ancient and both more or less derelict, but having an interest of their own. One is the church of SS. Quattro Coronati at the end of the Via of that name. These four saints were Severus, Severianus, Carpophorus and Victorinus, who were martyred under Diocletian. The church also venerates the memory of five sculptors who were put to death for refusing to make images of pagan deities, and it is therefore a place of pilgrimage for pious stone-cutters. Neither Canova nor Thorwaldsen seems to have enriched it, and to-day it is forlorn and neglected, one of its courts being used as a garage, and deaf-mutes having some kind of a hostel here. From the steep street beneath, the church rises in rather a fine mass. At the foot of the hill you see the Colosseum blocking the way.

We are also close to the curious structure S. Stefano Rotondo, a circular church with an inner circle of pillars, which under Nero was a meat market and must then have been more central than it now is. It is empty and forlorn, but a place of pilgrimage on account of the terrible frescoes on the walls depicting the awful ends of the Christian martyrs—an Italian version of Foxe's Book in paint. Here terrified children are brought to see St. Peter on his cross, St. Paul's decollation, St. John in the cauldron, St. Lawrence on his gridiron, St. Catherine on her wheel, and other horrors. The workmanship is poor.

I have spoken of S. Pietro in Vincoli, which of the

minor churches near the Colosseum is perhaps most visited. There is still one other of the greatest interest, and that is S. Clemente, in the street running direct from the Colosseum to the Lateran—the Via di S. Giovanni. The ancient kernel of S. Clemente is one of the daintiest and gayest things in Rome, with its two delicate pulpits, its pure and coloured marbles, its blue mosaic apse and cheerful mosaic patterns elsewhere among the white. But the restorers have done their best to give this lovely thing a garish setting. The ceiling is heavy with carving, the new aisles are commonplace, and a new chapel has been added in honour of SS. Cyril e Methodius, with frescoes by a French artist of the present day. As an antidote to these insipid works you must seek the Masaccios in another chapel and the kindly St. Christopher on the wall by the door, by some unknown early painter.

Beneath the church, on the level of the street, is another church dating from the fourth century, while beneath that is a subterranean Christian abode of the first century, in which St. Clement is thought to have lived. St. Clement, I should say, was a disciple of St. Peter and became the fourth Pope, his dates being 88-97. The residence under the church of SS. Giovanni e Paolo is perhaps more recognizably a home.

But the most striking of the buried pasts of this church is the pagan temple not long since revealed. For centuries water had lain in the foundations. A few years ago the pumps were set to work so that now the curious visitor may descend and reconstruct a sacrifice in perfection. I wonder if any Romans creep here at dark in honour of the old lost gods as the early Christians crept to the catacombs in honour of the new! When one reflects that the ruined condition of the Forum Romanorum is due to the vandal Popes who destroyed the beau-

THE COLOSSEUM

[*See page* 194

tiful buildings and covered them with rubbish in order that the Paganism which erected them should be dishonoured, there would be some piquancy in such midnight religious observances.

Chapter XX

The Lateran

Before the Vatican—Constantine the Great—Supernatural Allies
—St. Helena and the Holy Land—The Lateran Obelisk—The Bap-
tistery—A Sumptuous Church—The Twelve Apostles in their
Magnificence—A Giotto Fresco—Leo XIII—Innocent III—Martin
V—The Lateran Relics—Clement XII—The Lateran Museums—The
Scala Santa—S. Croce and its Relics.

THE commanding church of San Giovanni in Laterano
is one of the most memorable ecclesiastical buildings
in Rome and is best placed of all better even than St.
Peter's. St. Peter had to make his own site glorious;
but St. John found a lofty plain all to his hand. The
noble travertine façade, with its row of saints along the
coping, so strong and big and defiant in their rightness,
is on the heights of Monte Celio, looking due west. In
front of it the ground slopes down towards a new residential suburb; on the right is the ancient wall with the
busy Porta S. Giovanni at the foot, and the closed Porta
Asinorum where the inner galleries of the Aurelian Wall
may best be seen.

I made a comparison between St. John's and St. Peter's,
but really St. Peter's hardly deserves to be mentioned,
because of its youth and in a way its usurpation. For it
was here, at the Lateran, that the Popes first had their
dwelling and their temple. The Lateran was the Vatican
until in 1305 the papal abode was moved to Avignon. In
1377, when Gregory XI came back, persuaded to the
step by the intercession of St. Catherine of Siena, who
accompanied him, it was to the Vatican that he came, and
the Vatican has been the residence of the Popes ever since.

202

THE LATERAN

The imperial palace here was given to the Church by Constantine the Great. The son of St. Helena, that Emperor, although brought up at the court of Diocletian, was never a violent anti-Christian, and after he was guided to victory in one of his conflicts with Maxentius by the sign of a cross in the sky surrounded by the words "In this, conquer," he set the cross on his banner, gave his palace at the Lateran to the Pope of that day—Melchiades (311-314)—expressed his belief in Christianity and stopped the persecution of his newly acquired brethren. It is true that, for a while, he recanted sufficiently to allow persecution to be resumed, but on being stricken with leprosy he repented, sent for the new Pope, Sylvester I (314-335), and was baptized: dying in the new faith which before long was to be adopted by the State.

In the largest of the Stanze of Raphael in the Vatican —the Sala di Constantino—are the crowded, vivacious frescoes commemorating Constantine's conversion. Raphael drew them, but the painting was largely by his pupils. In one we see the Emperor aware of the cross in the sky; then he is in the thick of his battle with Maxentius, the success of Constantine's arms being assured by celestial commanders-in-chief directing the fight from the clouds, of whom, I assume, Maxentius was not also aware. And then Constantine's baptism.

A word about Constantine's mother, St. Helena, who is of interest to us because she was the daughter of a British ruler whom the nursery rhyme has made famous as Old King Cole. On becoming emperor, Constantine established his mother at Treves. She was not then a Christian, but after her son adopted the faith she followed him, and gave herself to piety and charity. In 325 she visited the Holy Land on a pilgrimage of expiation for her son's lapses as Emperor, and while there she excavated the cross from the soil of Calvary and found also the bodies of the

203

Three Magi and the seamless vest of Our Lord. On her return, she built the church of the Santa Croce where, as we shall see, some of these relics are preserved. Others are elsewhere, St. Peter's having a portion of the cross in the reliquary of St. Helena's pier supporting the Dome. At the Vatican we saw the wonderful porphyry sarcophagus of St. Helena and her husband, Constantius Chlorus, which came from her mausoleum outside Rome. St. Helena's present resting-place is in S. Maria in Aracœli.

A giant statue of Constantine, brought from his baths, stands in the entrance hall of the church; an obelisk erected by Constantine in the Circus Maximus is now in the neighbouring Piazza; and it was in the little circular Baptistery here that just in time the great Emperor washed away his paganism and his sins.

Of all the obelisks of Rome, this one at the Lateran is the largest. It has had a curiously mixed career, beginning in the fifteenth century B.C. as an ornament of the Temple of Ammon at Thebes; in course of time sailing for Europe and set up to decorate a Roman circus; then falling and lying in three pieces for centuries until, in the sixteenth century A.D., it was re-erected here, as an advance guard of a Christian church.

The Baptistery where, one day, I witnessed the simultaneous christening of two infinitesimal Romans, each, although of the tenderest age, with a shock of black hair, is a meeting-place of old building and less old. The earliest Baptistery in existence, and for long the only one in Rome (which suggests that the Christians clustered in this quarter), it provided the model, the reason why so many of the Baptisteries that we see are circular being because this one came first.

Constantine's church long since perished, the present basilica being the work of a series of Popes. Fire again

THE PORTA S. PAOLO, THE PYRAMID OF CESTIUS,
AND THE PROTESTANT CEMETERY

[*See page* 218

and again triumphed here, very beautiful things being destroyed, among them a series of frescoes by Giotto and another by Gentile da Fabriano. One Giotto still remains, as we shall see when we proceed through the building.

Within, S. Giovanni in Laterano could comfortably accommodate several English churches of importance and still have room over. On the day when I was last there a series of pilgrimages were in progress, the pilgrims singing as they moved, and the walls were rich with crimson. Normally the church is cold, but it has many splendours and the precious marbles in the apse are superb, the gift of Leo XIII (1878-1903), whose monument adjoins. The floor is purple with porphyry and the carved ceiling gorgeous with gold. The design has been attributed to Michael Angelo, but that other enricher of Rome, Giacomo della Porta, was more probably the artist. The Twelve Apostles in the nave are almost terrifying in their confident accomplishment and make one again wonder what those disseminators of the gospel of meekness and purity of heart really were like. Each has his symbol: St. Peter his key and book, St. Thomas his T square, St. John (clean shaven) his pen, book and eagle, St. Philip his cross and his foot on a dragon, St. Matthew reading his Gospel with a critical intensity, St. Bartholomew with his skin in a fold of his robe, and so forth.

Beginning with the right aisle, into which the Porta Santa leads, we find on the back of St. Matthew's pillar, on the left, the one remaining Giotto fresco, transferred here from its original site. It represents Boniface VIII proclaiming the first Jubilee in 1300. These Jubilees, or Holy Years (Anni Santi), have been held almost without interruption ever since, the period being shortened in the eighteenth century to twenty-five years. The Giottos that we saw in St. Peter's sacristy are more varied, but not more beautiful, than this, which has the lucidity and serenity of a fine sunset.

A rapid idea of the inferiority of later church painting in Rome may be obtained by comparing with the work of the pioneer Giotto the sophisticated frescoes, in the transept, of the life of Constantine, which are mediocre, while the altar paintings are frankly bad.

I have spoken of the precious coloured marbles of the tribune, which are recent, and are due to the interest in the church taken by Leo XIII. This humane and scholarly Pope, the friend of many distinguished Englishmen, Mr. Gladstone not least, reigned from 1878 to 1903, following Pio Nono.

To the right of the choir is the tomb of Innocent III (1198-1216) erected by Leo XIII several centuries later. Innocent III, a member of the Conti family, and nephew of Clement III, was one of the most forcible, practical and sagacious of all the long line of spiritual administrators. Most Popes, as a glance at the average brevity of their reigns will tell, have come to the throne at an advanced age. Indeed, as I have said, the spectacle of any great ceremony of the Roman Church conveys an impression of prevailing senescence. But Innocent III was elected at the age of only thirty-seven, and, in spite of that apparent disadvantage, quickly made his presence felt all over Europe. The Papacy, indeed, was never so powerful and the Lateran became a kind of Palace of the League of Nations. To give a notion of Innocent's strength, I have but to remind you that it was he who excommunicated both our King John and Philippe Auguste of France.

A third Pope's tomb in the Lateran is that of Martin V (1417-1431), a member of the Colonna family, often so anti-Papal, who gave the church its pavement. This noble bronze monument is in the floor of the Confessio before the Gothic canopy which, next to the relics, is perhaps San Giovanni's greatest pride. Within the altar beneath it are preserved the heads of St. Peter and St. Paul, and the table at which St. Peter used to say Mass. In the left transept is the actual table at which the Last Supper was eaten.

It was Martin V who was Pope during the Schism of Barcelona, when he had as rivals Clement VIII, the Spaniard (1423-1429)—nothing to do with Clement VIII of the true line, whose dates were 1592-1605—and Benedict XIV (1425-1430) who also must be separated from Benedict XIV (1740-1758). It was Martin V who first appointed the Swiss Guard at the Vatican, and much necessary rebuilding and restoration, including the Pantheon roof, was done by him. His tomb bears the words: "Temporum suorum felicitas": he was the good fortune, or happiness, of his times.

In the Corsini chapel, in the first aisle, is the tomb of Clement XII (1730-1740), a member of the powerful Corsini family. Although seventy-eight and bed-ridden when he was elected Pope, he was mentally active. To him was due the first issue of paper money in Italy—perhaps a doubtful boon. It was he also who began the Papal feud with the Freemasons. He added to the Vatican Library, and the frequency with which you see the words "Clement XII Pont. Max." over buildings shows that he had zeal for his city. You see them, for example, over the Fontana di Trevi.

The museums in the Lateran Palace adjoining this church are for the antiquary, the architect and the artist rather than for the uninstructed visitor, but no one should neglect them. In the Pagan section are many beautiful cornices, capitals and foliations; in the Christian section one may follow the vicissitudes of the secret believers in the days of their persecution, of which we shall see much more when we come to the catacombs. The sarcophagi with stories from the Old Testament—such as Jonah being swallowed and being rejected—are amusing. The place is usually deserted; Romans do not come here, nor do many tourists.

The building across the piazza to the left as one stands with one's back to San Giovanni contains the Scala Santa, the holy marble steps once a part of the palace of Pilate at Jerusalem and said to have been ascended and descended by Christ during His Passion. Brought here by St. Helena, they are now covered with wood and are ascended, on the knees only, both as an act of devotion and as a penance. At intervals, through glass, may be seen the marks of Christ's wounded feet. If I were Pope, I think I should consider the advisability of making the steps of Santa Maria in Aracœli a Scala Santa, instead of, or as well as, these, because so steep and so many and so public are they that ascending them would be a punishment indeed. No sin too dark to be thus expiated.

At the head of the Scala Santa is the Sancta Sanctorum, in which is preserved a picture of Christ, not painted by mortal hands. St. Luke is said to have made the outline and the rest was done by angelically guided brushes.

After the Lateran, we should go to Santa Croce in Gerusalemme, a short distance away between the Porta S. Giovanni and the Porta Maggiore. The Lateran church was Constantine's; Santa Croce, as I have said, was built by his mother on her return from the Holy Land. She had found all three crosses, ascertaining which was that of Christ by touching a sick person with each. Those on which the thieves were crucified had no effect; the other healed him. St. Helena found also the inscription on Christ's cross, thorns from the Crown of Thorns and some nails. In a little subterranean chamber at the

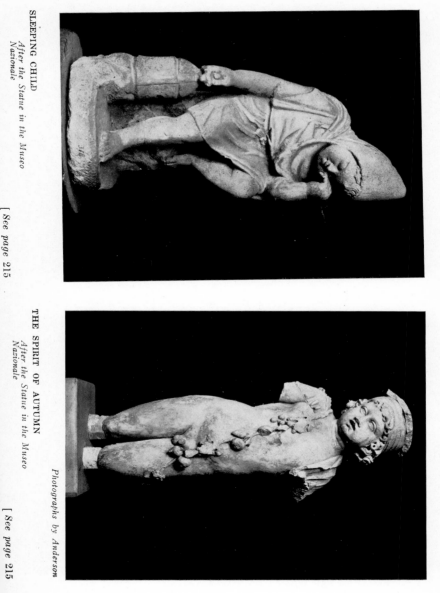

SLEEPING CHILD
After the Statue in the Museo Nazionale

[*See page* 215

THE SPIRIT OF AUTUMN
After the Statue in the Museo Nazionale

Photographs by Anderson

[*See page* 215

ATHLETE WITH STAFF
*After the Bronze Statue in
the Museo Nazionale*

[*See page* 215

THE LATERAN

church you are shown these relics, together with others, such as the doubting finger of St. Thomas. The monk who displays and describes them does not accept any monetary gift, but you are encouraged to buy rosaries and relics in the sacristy.

CHAPTER XXI

The Baths of Diocletian

S. Bernardo—The Aqua Felice—Strange Lapses from Reverence
—The two Susannas—S. Maria della Vittoria—The Via Venti Set-
tembre—The Porta Pia—S. Maria degli Angeli—Michael Angelo as
Architect—Houdon in Rome—S. Bruno's Statue—The Unconquerable
Roman Builder—The Venus of Cyrene—Michael Angelo's Cloisters—
The Treasures of the Terme of Diocletian—Roman Shops—Early
Plaster Reliefs.

HAD we left the Via Sistina at the Four Fountains
and turned to the left up the Via Venti Settembre
for a little way, past the Ministry of War, we should
have come to S. Bernardo standing back on the right;
a circular building, once a pavilion at one of the corners
of the Baths of Diocletian (whither we are tending), but
since 1600 a Christian church and now a favourite place
for baptisms. It is a very pleasant temple, with a domed
ceiling which is like the Pantheon's, except that it is made
not of diminishing squares but diminishing octagons.
Once a large monastery spread here; to-day there are
hotels.

At the corner of the Piazza S. Bernardo we find the
wall fountain known as the Aqua Felice, which takes its
name from Felice Peretti, who became Pope Sixtus V and
brought a supply of water hither from the Alban hills.
Most people think of it as the fountain of Moses, because
a figure of that patriarch, accompanied by Aaron and
Gideon, is there carved.

The façade once was plastered with posters, but Rome

210

is neater now and you see them only at the sides. In this matter of mural tidiness I am sorry to say that the Church does not set the city a good example, but every morning authorizes a new crop of notices of special services, pilgrimages and masses to break out at all angles on its fanes, utterly disregardful of the feelings of their architects—the Berninis and Madernas, the della Portas and Cortonas,—peering through the loopholes of Paradise. But the Church of Rome is seldom sensitive to incongruity or mindful of æsthetic harmonies. Having set the best artists in the world to work, it cheerfully obliterates that work or utterly discourages it by the cheapest and gaudiest hangings and the privation of all but dim artificial light. I was never so conscious of this want of feeling—probably the defect of a quality, that quality in the present instance being confidence—as in the crypt at San Lorenzo, where the altar before the beautiful and ancient tombs of St. Lawrence and St. Stephen was covered with a piece of white American cloth, and I noticed the same squalid material on the altar above Raphael's tomb.

On the opposite side of the street to S. Bernardo is the American Embassy and close to it the church of Santa Susanna, a Christian martyr with whom is associated another Susanna not yet canonized—Susanna of the Elders. Scenes in the lives of both Susannas are on the walls, the Apocryphal one being so heavily clad that the Elders leave the bath without a stain on their character. The other Susanna, a daughter of St. Sabinius, was beheaded in 292, under Diocletian, because she refused to marry a pagan kinsman of the Emperor. Vestiges of her father's house have been found below the church. Both her remains and her father's are in the Confessio.

In the chapel of St. Lawrence will be found frescoes illustrating the unusual story of two actors who became converts to Christianity and suffered martyrdom accordingly. They were canonized as St. Genesius and St. Eleutherius and their relics are preserved in the church.

A few yards from S. Susanna is Maria della Vittoria, one of the gayest little churches in Rome, every inch of it gold or colour or statuary, celebrating by its name the triumph of the Catholic Maximilian of Bavaria over the Lutheran Elector Palatine, at Prague, in 1620. This conquest was due to the influential presence on the battle-field of an image of the Virgin, an effigy which used to be honoured here, but has now perished. A modern fresco in the ceiling of the apse celebrates the event, but is rarely to be properly seen. The church is only a little more than three hundred years old. Bernini's famous St. Theresa group will be found here: more brilliant than pious; and here are paintings by Domenichino and Guercino. There was once a beautiful garden adjoining, where the Carmelites wandered and pondered and tended their flowers; but the Ministry of Agriculture has been built over it.

In a tiny green space adjoining, a lifesize figure of the Virgin is set, illuminated by night, for the comfort of passers-by.

If we continued our walk up the Via Venti Settembre we should come on the right to what in Whitehall would be called the Treasury. And, at the end, to the British Embassy, with its charming garden spreading away behind it, and the Villa Buonaparte, the home of Canova's Pauline, the naked princess, opposite; and then to Porta Pia and the Aurelian Wall once more.

The Porta Pia, named after Pius III, was designed by Michael Angelo, in his capacity as a martial architect, but its chief fame comes from the fact that it was here that the Italian soldiers, on September 20, 1870, forced their way into Rome and deprived it of its independence. You will see tablets commemorating the event and also

THE BATHS OF DIOCLETIAN

a column of victory just outside the gate. The Wall may be followed from here in one direction as far as the Porta del Popolo, passing the Porta Solaria and Porta Pinciana on the way, and in the other as far as the distant Porta San Paolo; but this would be a long excursion. Our objective this morning is the Baths of Diocletian.

The church of S. Maria degli Angeli, adjoining and absorbing the Baths, is famous chiefly for the immense size of its nave as Michael Angelo constructed it from the old tepidarium. In those days the main door was where the right transept altar now is, a later architect having turned the nave into the transept. The meridian of Rome crosses the pavement. The church, which is rather tawdry in its colouring and its painted marble among the real, and which seems larger and emptier than any in Rome, was an adjunct of the Carthusian convent ordained by Pius IV, of which Michael Angelo's cloisters are the chief beauty.

There are some bold and vigorous mural paintings, and in the choir two monuments by Michael Angelo, but the lodestar that takes me there is the giant figure of S. Bruno, founder of the Carthusian Order, by the gentle French sculptor Jean Antoine Houdon (1740-1828) who studied in Rome, the earthly paradise of all sculptors, as a young man. The S. Bruno is said to have been made when Houdon was only twenty, and although it is a colossal representation of the stern recluse, such was the innate tenderness of the artist that it is as charming in its way as those enchanting busts of children by the same hand in one of the ground-floor galleries of the Louvre. The statue delighted Clement XIV, who said of it that it could be called a speaking likeness but for the fact that the Saint's Order imposed a vow of silence. One other statue of S. Bruno that I recall in Rome is also good—sculptors apparently cannot do wrong when modelling

213

this benign creature—but not the equal of Houdon's. It is in St. Peter's, in a niche in the transept, and here again charm is a characteristic. The presence of a child adds a pretty emphasis.

The pictures of S. Maria degli Angeli are rather theatrical and of the decadent period. Two Italian artists once in higher favour than now were buried here and their tombs may be seen: Carlo Maratta, on the right as you enter, and Salvator Rosa on the left: names to conjure with two centuries ago.

I should remind you, before leaving the church, to look back from the altar through the entrance at the glittering fountain of the Naiadi.

For imparting an idea of the devotion of the ancient Romans to the pleasures of the bath, the Terme of Diocletian are inferior to those of Caracalla, which we shall visit later. There, the baths may be reconstructed by the intelligent eye; here the interest is in the sculptures that have been assembled.

The Museo Nazionale Romano in the Terme of Diocletian is supposed to confine itself to works of art found during excavations in Rome itself. Now and then, however, the rule has been broken. The most lovely thing, for instance, is the Aphrodite Anadyomene da Cyrene, a statue which is of Greek origin, probably of the fifth century B.C., discovered in Tripoli not many years ago and given this name. She has lost head and arms, but one soon ceases to think of that. She is less glorious than the Venus of Milo, but far more human than the Venus of the Capitoline. Her charm is irresistible, and, as I have said elsewhere, "in no other statue has the sculptor come so near the miracle of turning flesh to stone or stone to flesh."

I think I am more fond of this museum than of any in Rome. Not only because of the Venus, but because it is

THE BATHS OF DIOCLETIAN

so attractively placed, with Michael Angelo's beautiful dignified arches and windows all about; because it is a mixture of indoors and out, the gardens being full of flowers and sunshine; and because there is not too much to see. At the Vatican there is so much that the eye is fatigued. Sculpture can be very dazzling.

Whatever you miss at the Terme you must see the marble Venus and the bronze athlete, that superb straight figure holding a long staff and standing like one who knows his strength, fears none, but has no arrogance. You must see the marble head of the sleeping Fury, and the old pugilist in bronze so conscious that pugilists cannot be successful forever. You must see the beautiful groups in marble of Electra and Orestes, of Bacchus and a Satyr; and the single figures of Mars in repose, of "La Fanciulla d'Anzio," and of Calliope. These all have a touch, or more than a touch, of sublimity. Three other masterpieces of a lowlier cast, but each with so much charm, are the Roman girl with her coiled and plaited hair; the "Genius of Autumn," like one of Bacchus's little sons, with a cherubic face under his curls and a spray of grape-vine over his shoulder; and, perhaps above all, the poor little drowsy sentinel, in a hood and cloak, with his lantern at his side, who has dropped off to sleep at his post. Few collections of picture postcards brought away from Rome fail to include one of this "Fanciullo Addormentato."

Among the shops of Rome, those which sell picture postcards are very numerous; but stationery seems to be almost the principal commodity. Those old and strangely assorted companions, Salt and Tobacco, have their many strongholds, but bars are few. Fish shops, so interesting in foreign towns, you almost never see; but there is a big fish market in the Via S. Teodoro.

To return to the Terme, sculpture is not all. Up-

stairs will be found paintings on plaster removed bodily
from the walls of excavated villas, most delicately decora-
tive in their faded tints; and some exceedingly lovely
light reliefs, uncoloured, also from the houses of the rich
at Farnesina. Early though they be, they are so exquisite as to make most modern work in this medium, and
even some of the great Renaissance period, appear coarse.

THE VILLA UMBERTO I FROM THE PIAZZA DI SIENA

[*See page* 226

Chapter XXII

St. Paul and His Church

I SAID something in an early chapter about the Protestant cemetery, taking it out of its true place. The ordinary course for the traveller is to visit it on the way to S. Paolo fuori le Mura and the Tre Fontane, for it lies beside the pyramid of Cestius just outside the S. Paolo gate, once the Porta Ostiensis, leading to the Ostian Way and the great basilica of the apostle.

The road to St. Paul's is ugly and industrial, with factories and warehouses beside it. You see in the distance on the right the curious Monte Testaccio, which, though a mountain, is the work of man, being nothing but a rubbish heap formed by dumping here the fragments of earthen jars—wine jars, oil jars, water jars—for countless generations.

The story goes that both St. Paul and St. Peter were led, bound, to their fate along this road, but here again legend and history are inextricably mingled. That St. Paul was put to death at the Tre Fontane is a generally accepted statement, but St. Peter's martyrdom is placed elsewhere: by some high on the Janiculum, by others on a spot where the Vatican now stands. Anyway the two Apostles may have been in each other's company on the fatal day, which has been fixed for June 29, in either A. D.

66 or 67, under Nero, and the little chapel on the left of the Ostian Way, after the railway has crossed the road, is called the Chapel of the Parting and is associated with their farewell. St. Paul's words to St. Peter were "Peace be with thee, Foundation of the Church, Shepherd of the Flock of Christ," St. Peter replying "Go in peace, Preacher of Glad Tidings, Guide of the Just to Salvation." St. Peter would then have been taken to whatever spot his cross was waiting for him, and St. Paul led on to the headsman at the Tre Fontane.

I should say that the Three Fountains were not then heard of. The place where the Abbey of that name now stands was known as the Aquæ Salviæ. Why so distant a spot should have been chosen, I cannot explain, unless some revolt was feared. It is the more strange because Nero is said to have wished to witness the decapitation, and a cell is shown under the church of S. Maria Scala Cœli in which the Apostle was confined until the Emperor arrived. There is also a fresco depicting the scene with the Emperor as an onlooker—as he had been when Simon Magus attempted his miracle and perished. According to the legend, when St. Paul's head was struck off it fell and bounded three times, and at each spot where it touched earth a fountain gushed forth.

The churches at the Tre Fontane are those of St. Paul himself, the two saints Vincenzo and Anastasio, and S. Maria Scala Cœli. The Holy Stairs which give their name to the last were seen in a vision by St. Bernard, with souls liberated from Purgatory ascending them. You will find a representation of his dream over the altar. St. Vincent, a Spaniard, and St. Anastasius, a Persian, were both put to death for the Faith. The third church at the Three Fountains—that of St. Paul—was built on the site of his execution, and the three springs still bubble beneath it. The column to which he was bound is there too.

ST. PAUL AND HIS CHURCH

The Trappist monks, to whom the abbey belongs, make a liqueur or cordial of which the basis is eucalyptus. No harm in it.

But we have been advancing too fast. The Tre Fontane are some distance beyond the great church which we came especially to see, and they ought to have been described last. Since, however, they bring the actual life of St. Paul to an end, the disorder is perhaps justified, especially as the church contains his tomb; and we will now see that majestic fane, where his remains are preserved and his name is honoured, as, in London, it is honoured in the commanding cathedral on Ludgate Hill.

The body of St. Paul was buried by his devout followers in the vineyard of a Roman Christian lady named Lucina, and within a few years a chapel was built over the tomb by Pope Cletus, or St. Anacletus (76-88), who similarly built over the tomb of St. Peter the chapel which, in spite of renovations, still is the very core of his church, containing the most sacred relics there, as anyone descending to the Confessio may see. Similarly, at the great church of St. Paul, although many have been the changes, the remains of the Apostle are still in the Confessio beneath the high altar.

Both at St. Peter's and St. Paul's, I should say, the early reverential memorial chapels built by Pope Anacletus were made splendid, two and a half centuries later, by Constantine the Great. Thereafter Emperors and Popes vied with each other to enlarge and beautify them.

I have referred to St. Paul's in London. The difference in situation between that cathedral and St. Paul's-outside-the-walls of Rome is very striking, for whereas our St. Paul's is on a high point in the midst of crowded streets, the Roman St. Paul's is isolated among marshy fields. It is the most surprising building that I know. For two miles you are proceeding along this half-deserted and utterly hideous Ostian Way, having left behind you only as a memory the wonderful city of people and palaces and architectural sophisticalism, and then suddenly you find yourself in a church more vast, more glorious, than any. I say more vast, but that may be inaccurate. What I mean is, that it appears to be more vast. This is partly due to the fact that you see so much of it at once, whereas both St. Peter's and our own St. Paul's disclose themselves only piecemeal, with aisles and transepts hidden by columns and piers. As a matter of fact St. Paul's in Rome is only one hundred and thirty-nine yards in length (but think of a hundred yards race and how long that can be, and then think of it a third longer and enclosed by rows of magnificent granite columns under a ceiling of splendour), whereas St. Peter's is two hundred and five yards and St. Paul's in London one hundred and seventy-three. But the openness of S. Paolo fuori, the emptiness of it, and the regularity of its myriad pillars, make it seem incredibly immense; an effect heightened, as I have said, by its unexpectedness in that desolate region. Perhaps its outer columned courtyard, through which the main façade is approached, and which also is of an immensity, adds further to the impression of size.

Although the inception of the church dates from the first century A.D., the imposing building that we now see is of the nineteenth century and is one of the most considerable enterprises of the Church of Rome in recent memory. For in 1823 the structure representing the early efforts of St. Anacletus, of Constantine the Great, of Valentinian II, of Theodosius, of Honorius, and of Pope Leo III, together with additions and enrichments innumerable, was destroyed by fire. Here is a mystery of mysteries which confronts one in almost every church that has ever been burnt; and Rome is full of them. How does one set light to a church? And, even more so, how does

ST. PAUL AND HIS CHURCH

one ignite a church without pews? What is there that is inflammable? Stone is not, nor marble, nor bronze, and little else is to be seen.

Be that as it may, St. Paul's was burned, and not until 1854 was its successor ready for consecration, by Pius IX. And then in 1891 came a powder explosion to damage it again and break every window. If any church could be thought safe, it would be this one, isolated and unfrequented; but no.

In spite of the fire and the explosion, the church has many relics of early times and of the Middle Ages. The canopy over the high altar belongs to the thirteenth century and may be by Arnolfo di Cambio, of the Duomo in Florence; and there are also mediæval mosaics. But one thinks of it as a new church, and, like the tribune of the Lateran and the Vittorio Emmanuele II Memorial, a further proof of what the recent Roman builder can do, and what treasures the quarries of Italy still possess.

Chapter XXIII

The Villa Umberto I

The Villa Borghese—Rome's Bois de Boulogne—Napoleon's Sister as Venus—Giovanni Lorenzo Bernini—The Daphne—The Rape of Proserpine—The pious Æneas—The Picture Gallery—Correggio's Danaë—Titian's Sacred and Profane Love—Paul Veronese—The Roman Zoo—The Law against Tips—The National Gallery of Rome —Modern Art—Verdi and Boldini.

THE Villa Borghese, as it used to be called—now the Villa Umberto I—can be gained from the Piazza di Spagna steps and from the Piazza del Popolo, through the Pincio. But nowadays, when the Anglo-Saxon residential tide has set towards the Ludovisi quarter, most foreigners enter it by the Porta Pinciana in the Aurelian Wall, at the top of the Via Veneto. On the gate is a memorial to the Ludovisi men who died in the Great War.

Immediately on the left on entering is the Rotten Row of Rome, where officers in blue gallop with pretty women, and a little way along the road that skirts it is the Goethe memorial with symbolical figures around it, which the Emperor William presented to Rome in 1904, when all was peace. For French hero-worshippers there is a statue of Victor Hugo, erected a year later, beside the road to the Popolo.

The Villa covers many acres of grass and woodland, with an old race-course in the midst called the Piazza di Siena, and a Zoo in the far corner, while statues and fountains and picturesque ruins occur in the true classical manner of Wilson and Claude.

222

THE VILLA UMBERTO I

The word Villa, I should say, covers the whole estate. The residence was called the Casino, and this Casino, where the art collections are preserved, is notable all the world over for a few paintings and many very beautiful works in marble and precious stone. Its first owner, Cardinal Scipione Borghese, built this country home at the beginning of the seventeenth century and began the collections. A later head of the family, Prince Marc-antonio Borghese, rebuilt it in 1782 and added to the treasures, many of which were looted by Napoleon in 1807 and have never come back. The present collection was formed by Prince Camillo Borghese, who married Napoleon's sister Pauline; and the Villa and everything on it became the property of the State in 1901.

The entrance hall is notable for the very fine Dionysus on the right and a dancing faun opposite. In the first little room on the right is the famous half-draped Pauline Borghese, as Venus, by Canova. Why this work should have created such a sensation it is difficult to realize, for it is perfectly decorous and, to many eyes, not excluding mine, is insipid. The delicate pattern on the edge of the marble couch is more attractive than the figure. A portrait of Canova is kept on an easel near by.

The next room has Bernini's figure of David about to let loose his sling. The sculptor is said to have been only eighteen when this work was accomplished, and the story goes that his own face is reproduced as that of the shepherd boy, Cardinal Maffeo Barberini, his first patron, afterwards Urban VIII (1623-1644) often holding the mirror while the portrait was in progress. David's body strikes me as being older than that of the shepherd stripling at whom Goliath laughed, while the head is rather too small; but the statue has much spirit.

Since we shall see so much of Bernini's work here, and are constantly meeting with it in Rome, a few words as to his career may be welcome. He is, in fact, constantly asserting himself, whether as an architect of churches and palaces, acting independently; as an architect of churches and palaces, rounding off the work of other men; as a sculptor, rather florid in style, but with a fine urgency, and a sufficiently diverse method to make not only these Borghese groups, but also the angels of the Passion on the Castel Sant' Angelo bridge, and the St. Theresa at Santa Maria della Vittoria; as a painter; and not least as a designer of fountains. It is, indeed, his fountains that give him his special place in Rome, for without them the city would lack much of its charm.

Giovanni Lorenzo Bernini was a Neapolitan by birth, born in 1598. He began as a painter, and we shall find upstairs his own self-portrait—a sad, distinguished countenance, in the manner of Velasquez, whom he almost certainly met in Rome in 1630 and 1649. Later he developed great skill as a modeller of busts: so much so that Charles I sent Van Dyck out to Italy with his famous portrait taken from three points of view for a bust to be made from it. Bernini died richer than any artist of his time, leaving, in 1680, over £100,000.

In addition to the David in this second little room there are charming figures, the little boy with a club (LXXXIV), and the old man, perhaps Hercules, with a lion's skin (LXXXVI), on whom much Roman rain has fallen. This is one of the many terminal figures which must have made the gardens and allotments of the past so attractive.

In the next room is Bernini's Daphne, executed when he was twenty-four, for his second patron, Cardinal Scipione Borghese. In spite of the dictum, in which I believe, that sculpture should deal with completed action and repose, there can be no doubt that this is a brilliant rendering of so incomplete an act as the transformation of a

DANAË
After the picture by CORREGGIO *in the Borghese Gallery*

[*See page* 226

Photograph by Anderson

SACRED AND PROFANE LOVE
After the Picture by TITIAN in the Borghese Gallery

[See page 226

lady into a tree. Look also for the two little imps milking a goat.

The next room, a magnificent hall, is a palace of porphyry. The Emperors are here, their massive features cut from that imperial Egyptian rock. There is a wonderful porphyry bath, and there are porphyry tables bearing basalt urns. Vases of translucent marble are in the windows and twenty columns of oriental alabaster may be marvelled at. The principal statue is again Bernini's —the Rape of Proserpine by Pluto. "Tears, that invincible feminine argument," says the official catalogue in its English form, "have not been neglected by Bernini: two tears run down the left cheek of the weeping virgin enhancing the sweet charm of that beautiful visage." A little sleeping Cupid in basalt and a young Bacchus in marble should be looked for.

In the next room is the Hermaphrodite, without which no Continental museum of sculpture is complete. The Roman girl of many centuries ago (CLXXXI) I am sure I have met recently in England. The boy extracting a thorn is a copy of the famous original at the Capitoline.

The Bernini in the next room is fabled to have been executed when the artist was only fifteen. It represents the pious Æneas fleeing from Troy, bearing his father on his shoulders and leading the small Ascanius. Here again the sculptor has chosen for perpetuation a moment of great activity. There is a probability that Bernini's father assisted his son in this work. According to the catalogue, the young Ascanius carrying a lantern, whose connection with Rome is narrated in the chapter on the Capitoline, "symbolises the power of innocence which guides men on their way to salvation." The actual "Sleep of Innocence," by the way, may be studied in the group of three intertwined cupids (CLXXXIV), which you will see reproduced in Rome's many printshops. I like the two little figures on each side of this group: one with a bird (CXV) and one crying (CXIII). And the Sleeping Cupid (CVIII) is charming.

In the next room are more vessels of precious marbles, basalt and alabaster, and a rich mosaic floor in which porphyry predominates. The boy and the dolphin in the middle control the room.

The last of the ground-floor rooms has the famous Dancing Faun. There is rather a pretty group opposite (CCXXXXI) of a child with a dove beside a god. And Nos. CCXXVI and CCXXXII, both fauns or satyrs, but very harmless ones, have the easy postures and grace of which the eye never tires.

We now ascend to the picture rooms: if we are wise, entering a tiny lift for that purpose. The pictures, I may say at once, are chiefly of the declining period in Italian art. The gods having gone, the half-gods arrived. But they were not lacking worshippers, the chief of them in this collection—Domenichino—achieving in his day a popularity far beyond that of many a superior predecessor. The picture before which the guides who lead hither English and American lambs to the slaughter pause longest, and are most voluble, is Domenichino's "Chase of Diana," prized, says the catalogue, by its owner, Cardinal Scipione Borghese, above all his artistic treasures. I do not deny its brilliancy, but it is the kind of picture that on me has little hold. Compared with Correggio's "Danaë" in another room it is almost negligible. This Danaë is glorious, another of its irresistible painter's conquests; but one needs better authority than the Catalogue for the daring statement that the model for Danaë was a Benedictine nun at the convent of St. Paul at Parma.

It is because of the Correggio and Titian's "Sacred and Profane Love" that the gallery is essential to art students; and of the Titian what can one say? Whether as a composition of sheer beauty, with no reference to its title (which may be a post-Titian idea), or whether as a rich and tender landscape with figures, it is equally notable. Its colour gradually fills the eyes and remains there.

The collection as a whole reflects a shallow material mind, but among the pictures that remain is a fine imaginative work attributed to Veronese in which the solitary figure of St. Anthony of Padua is seen preaching to a vast wilderness. This almost alone, among hundreds of facile studio productions, has imagination.

The visitor, however, should look for works by Perugino (No. 401), Palamedes, a portrait (No. 557), Antonella da Messina (No. 396), Raphael (?) (No. 397), Bellini (No. 176), El Greco (No. 365), very interesting; Carpaccio (?) (No. 450); and Savoldo (No. 547). And Bernini's portrait of himself must not be neglected.

Writing under oath as a F.Z.S. I cannot give the Rome Zoo absolutely full marks, but it is a very pleasant resort and the Italians love it, lavishing their attention and affection impartially upon elephants, of which there were two when I last saw it, and guinea pigs, the number of which it is never safe at any given moment to compute. The pond for water-fowls is quite as attractive as anything in Regent's Park or the Bronx, and the polar bears have an ideal residence; but the lions are poorly housed. Among the eagles I found two the gift of S. E. Benito Mussolini. Many wolves from the Abruzzi are there, for the cage at the Capitol to be recruited from when necessary. The Orario dei Pasti gives from twelve till half-past three as the monkeys' eating time; but I saw an extension in progress.

One bad custom at the Roman Zoo is an extra charge both for these Scimmie and for the Casa dei Rettili. As in London, the happiest animal seems to be the otter, here called a lontra; but nothing could exceed the playfulness of a young puma and young hyena frolicking in the same cage, who now, I fear, have both settled down to the normal Zoological Gardens apathy.

Beyond the Villa Umberto I and the Zoo is the Valle Giulio, in which are the Villa Giulio and also two new white buildings: the British School of Art in Rome, and the National Gallery of Modern Italian Art. Above the British School is some waste grass land with a view of Rome and the aqueduct on Monte Mario against the sky; and here you may see Italian cavalrymen from the neighbouring barracks doing astonishing things on horseback, up and down the slopes.

Tips, in Government buildings, are authoritatively forbidden in Italy ("è abolita la mancia"), although, habit dying hard, hands can still be outstretched; but nowhere is the notice against them so firm as at the National Gallery of Modern Italian Art, where it says, at the door, "Visitors giving any will be requested to leave the premises." But I have my doubts. As to this abolition of tips in hotels and the substitution of a 10 per cent. tax, I am not sure that I do not like the old way best. Leaving an hotel can, I admit, be a rather costly or humiliating experience when strange faces wear an expectant look; but the sum thus given might be generous and yet well beneath the 10 per cent. addition to a bill, while at any rate one is being bidden farewell. Under the new régime, all interest in you having evaporated, your departure is no longer an event, and you creep into the omnibus conscious of having made no one happy.

The National Gallery pictures are in the main defiantly able. Rarely do they touch any emotion. I liked the vivid *vraisemblance* of Boldini's pastel head of Verdi, whose compositions are still the most popular ingredients

of every orchestral programme. As some one has re-
marked, Italians don't really like music; they like Italian
music. This is no depreciation of Verdi, for I am with
them in this devotion, even though mine is not so exclusive
of the melody of other nationalities. Similarly I found
more to admire in the big cosmopolitan room at the gallery than in the many that were solely "du pays." But
the Segantinis I remember with pleasure, and some in-
teriors by Gioacchino Toma, and some Alpine villages by
Ramponi. The chief work of statuary is Canova's Hercules from the Palazzo Torloni, but a group called
Maternity, by Antonio Maraini, remains sweetly in the
memory.

Chapter XXIV

The Appian Way and the Catacombs

The Baths of Caracalla—An immense Club—*Prometheus Unbound*
—S. Balbina and S. Saba—SS. Nereo ed Achilleo—St. Peter's
Bandage—The Meeting of St. Lawrence and Pope Sixtus II—A
willing Martyr—The Tomb of the Scipios—The Arch of Drusus
—The Temple of Mars and the Last Chance—The Appian Way—
Christ's final Rebuke to St. Peter—The Catacombs of Rome—
Cemeteries and Conventicles—S. Callixtus and his Catacombs—Many
early Popes—S. Cecilia—Inscriptions and Symbols—The Church of
St. Sebastian—St. Peter and St. Paul—St. Sebastian's Martyrdom.

THE Baths of Caracalla may present a problem to
the visitor until he realizes the character of this
gigantic building. Why should baths, he would ask, even
when built by Emperors in love with vastness and magnificence, need such acreage of space? The answer is, that
they were not only baths, but comprised every accessory
of comfort and luxury. Every kind of bath, hot and
cold, was there, and also reading rooms, meeting rooms,
perhaps a theatre and concert hall, a gymnasium and so
forth. Even a race-course all round. The bath was a
recreation as well as a splendid ritual. Some of the most
beautiful works of sculpture now preserved were found
here, proving that the decoration was also imperial.

To wander among these crumbling walls is almost to
get a new idea of Roman magnificence; and I like to remember that it was here that Shelley, in 1819, wrote Acts
II and III of *Prometheus Unbound*.

The church on the hill above the Baths of Caracalla is
S. Balbina, named in honour of a Christian virgin who

was martyred under Hadrian, together with her father,
S. Quirinus, a tribune. Behind this church is the monastery of S. Saba, a far more beautiful retreat, with its
quiet cloisters and views of Rome. The original church
was the cell to which S. Sylvia, the mother of Gregory the
Great, retired after the death of her husband; much rebuilding has been done since and the place belongs now to
the German College, whose students are often seen dotting
the hillside with red.

The two churches nearer the Baths, one on each side
of the Via di Porta S. Sebastiano, are—close to the
baths—SS. Nereo ed Achilleo, and—opposite it—S. Sisto.
The former church was named after two martyrs, officers
of the Emperor Domitian's household, who are said to
have been converted by St. Peter in person. Their remains, after certain vicissitudes, are preserved here; all
but the heads, which are kept at S. Maria in Vallicella.
A passage from Gregory the Great's homily on the two
saints, pronounced in the catacombs of Domitilla, will be
found on the episcopal throne, supported by lions. An
earlier name for the church was Titulus de Fasciola, in
honour of the bandage which St. Peter is said to have
dropped from his foot, at this spot, as he was fleeing from
Rome, before the incident commemorated in the question
Quo vadis?

The other church of S. Sisto is the traditional place of
the meeting of St. Lawrence with Pope Sixtus II and his
four companions on their way to martyrdom. I borrow
from Father Chandlery's book the conversation that
passed between them.

St. Lawrence, then a young archdeacon, falling on his
knees, said to the Pope: "Father, where are you going
without your son? Whither are you going, O holy priest,
without your deacon? You were never wont to offer
sacrifice without me, your minister. Wherein have I dis-

pleased you? Have you found me wanting in my duty? Try me now and see whether you have made choice of an unfit minister for dispensing the Blood of the Lord?"

To which the Pope replied: "I do not leave you, my son, but a greater trial and a more glorious victory are reserved for you; you will follow me in three days' time." And so it fell out.

The convent of S. Sisto was given to S. Dominic by Pope Honorius III in 1217, and here the founder of the Dominican Order lived and performed miracles.

The next church, on the right as we advance nearer the Porta S. Sebastiano, is S. Cesareo, named after a martyr who perished under Diocletian in 300. Neither headsman nor lion, neither the cross nor the flames accounted for this valiant witness: he was tied in a sack with another priest and flung into the sea.

On the left of the road is the first of the tombs—that of the Scipios, the principal treasure of which, the sarcophagus of L. Cornelius Scipio Barbatus, consul in 298 B.C., we saw in the Vatican. Close by is the Columbarium of Pomponius Hylas, which is not a dove-cote at all but a repository for urns containing the ashes of the cremated.

Just before we reach the gate of St. Sebastian we pass through the Arch of Drusus, first erected, it is said, in 8 B.C., in honour of Drusus, stepson of Augustus, and his victories over the Germans, and then used as a support for the aqueduct bringing water to Caracalla's baths. But antiquaries differ. Anyway, the arch is, and is furthermore a fine memorial of building and design under the early Emperors.

The Porta S. Sebastiano, in the Aurelian Wall, is supposed to be constructed of materials brought from the ruined Temple of Mars, close by. There were once, around Rome, three hundred and eighty-three wall-towers like these. It was at the Temple of Mars, just outside

THE TOMB OF CECILIA METELLA ON THE APPIAN WAY

[*See page* 232

the gate, that the fettered Christians on their way to martyrdom were halted and given a last chance to renounce the new faith and be free again.

We are now in the Appian Way, a road constructed as long ago as 312 B.C., from Rome to the south and even to the sea, and taking its name from the consul Appius Claudius Cæcus. At first it is enclosed by walls; then it becomes more open. It was on either side that the Romans had their tombs, remains of which are still to be seen in some numbers, but only in fragments. With memories of the Street of Tombs at Pompeii in mind an imaginary reconstruction is easy.

Apart from its general interest, its antiquity, its ruins, its tombs, there are two special motives that take visitors to Rome along the Appian Way, and these are to see the Catacombs and to see the church known as the *Quo Vadis?* where again we come to St. Peter as actually a resident of Rome.

The story is, that when in the year 65 Nero's persecution of the Christians was at its height, St. Peter was persuaded to fly from the city. As he passed along the Appian Way he met, at the precise spot, Christ.

"Domine, quo vadis?" said St. Peter in astonishment: "Lord, whither goest Thou?"

"I go," Christ replied, "to Rome—to be crucified anew," and vanished.

The reproof in these words St. Peter could not misunderstand; he turned back and accepted his fate.

The story gains nothing from the traces of one of Christ's footprints in the stone, which is shown on the floor of the church, in an enclosing framework; particularly as this footprint is merely a replica, the church of St. Sebastian, further along the Via Appia, claiming to possess the original.

The galleries of the catacombs of Rome are said to

extend, in the aggregate, to nearly six hundred miles, or about twice the distance from Milan to Rome; but only a small section is shown. Most of this incredible space was devoted to burials, the early Christians resorting to secrecy through fear of the violation of their tombs and consequent frustration of the actual corporeal resurrection in which they believed. As we saw at the Columbarium of Pomponius Hylas, the custom of the pagan Romans was to be cremated; a custom which latter-day Christians are holding more and more in favour; but at that time burial was the rule with members of the new religion.

The catacombs served a second purpose in providing secret meeting-places where the devout might worship unmolested. In the very early days the faithful met more or less openly in the houses of the more powerful and highly placed converts. But when the persecutions began, there was need for stealth.

Of the many catacombs around Rome, those which have been most carefully prepared for sight-seers, and therefore are most visited, are the catacombs of S. Callixtus, St. Sebastian, and S. Domitilla, all on, or near, the Appian Way. As we come first to those of S. Callixtus, let us begin there.

S. Callixtus, whom we found in high honour at S. Maria in Trastevere, where his remains are preserved, was Pope from 217 to 229, being before his election superintendent of the cemetery that now bears his name. He was put to death under Alexander Severus.

A Trappist monk acts as guide, providing each visitor with a candle, and the descent begins at once. Thereafter one is led as in a trance, up and down, left and right, through passages lined with cavities in which masses of bones now and then are seen, broadening out here and there into frescoed chapels. The principal chapel in the

APPIAN WAY AND THE CATACOMBS

S. Callixtus catacombs is that of the Popes, many of the early Popes, most of them martyred, being buried here: from S. Soterus (166-175) and S. Zephyrinus (199-217) to S. Eutychianus (275-283) and S. Caius (283-296). The famous inscription of the poet S. Damasus, who was Pope from 366 to 384, is to be seen over the site of the altar beneath the frescoed lunette. "Here," say the concluding lines, in Latin, "Here I, Damasus, wished to have laid my limbs, but feared to disturb the ashes of the saints." The fresco depicts Christ among cherubim.

But popular interest centres in the chapel of S. Cecilia, where there is a replica of Maderna's statue in the church of that saint in Trastevere.

On the walls of the galleries are inscriptions poignant in their simplicity and affection. "Dear Cyriaco, sweetest of sons, mayest thou live in the Holy Spirit." "Christina, for believing in God and Christ, is with the angels." "Atticus, thy spirit is in bliss, pray for thy parents." These are typical. There is also an epitaph on a husband and his wife, stating roundly that they never had a single difference, although married for many years, which calls from the Trappist a punctual sardonic murmur.

Among the symbols we note the frequency of the lamb and the dove, which typify the faithful and the soul. A fish signifies Christ, a peacock eternity, the serpent evil, and so forth, as the Trappist will explain.

Meanwhile the air is getting stuffier, and the circumstance that your candle now and then drips on the sightseer ahead of you, makes you the more sure that the candle of the sight-seer behind is dripping on to you. But there is no escape until the guide has completed his appointed round. United, you have a chance; divided, you would be lost for ever, buried alive.

The catacombs of St. Sebastian, a little farther on, draw perhaps more pilgrims than those of S. Callixtus, by reason of the footprint of Christ in the church, and of the association, real or supposed, with St. Peter and St. Paul. The story has it that this church was built over the dry well in which the bodies of St. Peter and St. Paul were hidden, after their execution, before they could be given proper respect. The tomb of St. Sebastian is in the present church, in the first chapel on the left, with some realistic sculpture.

Recent excavators at the adjoining catacombs of St. Sebastian have revealed an underground dwelling which is confidently said to be the abode of St. Peter and St. Paul, with a pool for the baptismal rites beneath it. The enthusiastic monk who leads you with a candle through the labyrinthine graveyard, who speaks English, and who was himself one of the excavators, has not a shadow of doubt about it. No cicerone could be more solicitous than this friendly soul: "Christians buried; Romans cremated," he says at intervals, as he pauses to point to bones. "Bebby," he says, when a smaller niche than usual is passed, and, continually and comfortingly, "No step, lady; no step, gentleman."

A word as to St. Sebastian himself. This martyr, one of the most illustrious saints of the Church of Rome, whose day is January 20, is thought to have been a Roman soldier, born in Milan. Having secretly become a Christian, he converted his fellow soldiers, and also was effective in stimulating other Christians who now and then, knowing the risks, found themselves weakening. For this offence Sebastian was condemned by Diocletian to be shot by archers, at—if the Old Masters are to be believed—very short range. Short though the range was, the arrows did not kill and their victim was nursed back to life by one Irene, a holy woman. On his recovery he went to the Emperor to warn him of his ways, and was promptly sentenced to be beaten to death with rods.

That was in 288. Another holy woman, Lucina, finding the body, was told by the saint, in a vision, that he wished to be buried in the catacombs and that a church must be built over him. In the year 826 his remains were removed to Soissons, but his spirit still marches on the Appian Way.

CHAPTER XXV AND LAST

Apologies—Surrounding Towns and Lakes—Tivoli—The Villa Doria Pamphili—The Ponte Molle—The Aventine Hill—The Keyhole Vista—The Fontana di Trevi—A Final Duty.

REVIEWING our steps I find that I have omitted almost as much as I have included. So many ruins neglected, so many churches unvisited, and literally thousands of statues treated with total disregard. I take refuge in the fact that no one book could do justice to Rome, and that there was no promise to be exhaustive. One book may suffice to kindle enthusiasm for Rome, but only a library can explain her.

If I have said almost nothing about Rome outside her walls, the reason is that the plan of this book excluded it. But what a wonderful theme for another book—the churches and villas just outside, and then the Campagna itself, with its broken arches and forgotten temples, and then the surrounding towns: Albano, with its ancient crater, now an opal lake; Ginzano, with its viaduct and the Pontine marshes below and the strip of wine-dark sea across the sullen flatness; Nemi, with its ancient crater, now a sapphire lake; Rocco di Papa, with its sylvan sides, and the distant view of Rome from its summit—Rome being merely St. Peter's dome; Frascati with its sunny white retreats.

I am speaking only of the south. In the north is Bracciano, with its vaster lake, and all the little towns in the Tiber valley; in the east is Tivoli, with the Villa d'Este, that sombre paradise of murmuring waterways and silent giant cypresses, Tivoli with its cataracts and its

238

temples and Hadrian's villa, whose ruined courts, where the Emperor may or may not have drunk deep, the official custodian and the lizard now keep.

But these resorts are far afield. I have said nothing of the Roman villas on the very outskirts: the beautiful Villa Doria Pamphili on the Janiculum, with its lawns and altars, its stone pines and its silver pheasants, just as Decamps painted it in the Wallace collection; I have said nothing of the Villa Albani beyond the Porta Salaria, with its collections of antiques formed by that strange fastidious neo-Greek, Winckelmann. We have been a little way outside the Porta S. Sebastiano and the Porta S. Paolo and the Porta Pinciana; but those are all. I have said nothing of the Ponte Molle over the Tiber outside the Porta del Popolo, a bridge dating from 109 B.C., or of the Villa Madama, near it, which Raphael designed for Cardinal Giulio de' Medici (afterwards Pope Clement VII), and which another Giulio, the painter Giulio Romano, Raphael's pupil, decorated.

I have said almost nothing of the church of St. Agnes outside the Porta Pia, where Constantine the Great's daughter has her chapel and beneath which many Christians were buried. We have not yet climbed to the old churches on the steep winding ways, between walls, of the Aventine hill—to S. Prisca and S. Sabina and S. Maria Aventina—nor eaten at the Castle of the Cæsars, nor peered through the keyhole of the garden of the Knights of Malta, along the avenue, to the dome of St. Peter's so magically suspended in the sky at the end of the vista.

All these things are yet to do and I envy you the enlargement of the Roman adventure which this chapter is perhaps prompting.

Meanwhile I must stop, and I hope I have been of service. But before you too leave Rome for England

again, or for America again, or for the Dominions, you
have, you remember, one duty which must at any cost be
performed: you must throw a coin into the waters of the
Fontana di Trevi.

INDEX

INDEX

242

INDEX

243

INDEX

INDEX

245

INDEX

INDEX

INDEX

INDEX

249

INDEX

INDEX

251

INDEX

252

INDEX

INDEX

INDEX

INDEX

256

INDEX

257

INDEX

INDEX

259

INDEX

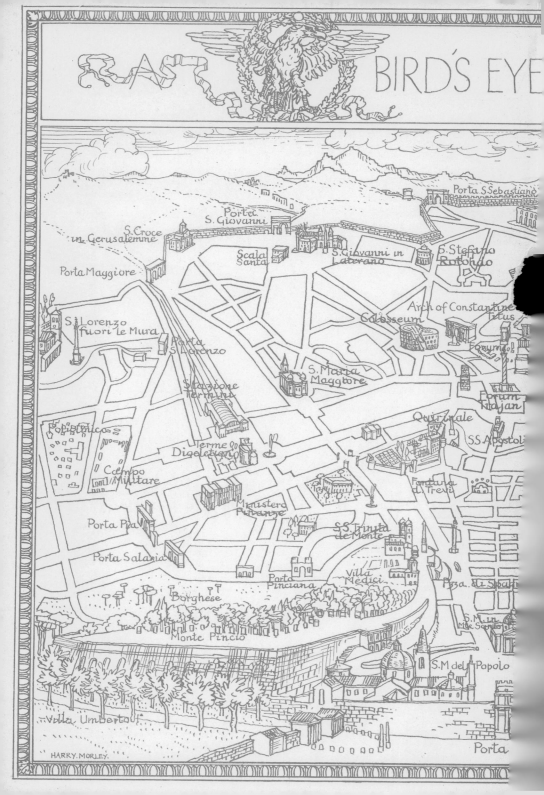